# MORE PSYCHOMETRIC TESTING

## Titles in *The IQ Workout Series*

Psychometric Testing: 1000 ways to assess your personality, creativity, intelligence and lateral thinking 0-471-52376-3

Increase Your Brainpower: Improve your creativity, memory, mental agility and intelligence 0-471-53123-5

IQ Testing: 400 ways to evaluate your brainpower 0-471-53145-6

More IQ Testing: 400 new ways to release your IQ potential 0-470-84717-4

Maximize Your Brainpower: 1000 new ways to boost your mental fitness 0-470-84716-6

*The IQ Workout Series*

# MORE PSYCHOMETRIC TESTING

1000 new ways to assess your personality, creativity,
intelligence and lateral thinking

Philip Carter and Ken Russell

**WILEY**

Published in 2003 by John Wiley & Sons Ltd, The Atrium, Southern Gate, Chichester,
West Sussex PO19 8SQ, England

Telephone    (+44) 1243 779777
Email (for orders and customer service enquiries): cs-books@wiley.co.uk
Visit our Home Page on www.wileyeurope.com or www.wiley.com

***Other Wiley Editorial Offices***

John Wiley & Sons Inc., 111 River Street, Hoboken, NJ 07030, USA

Jossey-Bass, 989 Market Street, San Francisco, CA 94103-1741, USA

Wiley-VCH Verlag GmbH, Boschstr. 12, D-69469 Weinheim, Germany

John Wiley & Sons Australia Ltd, 33 Park Road, Milton, Queensland 4064, Australia

John Wiley & Sons (Asia) Pte Ltd, 2 Clementi Loop #02-01, Jin Xing Distripark, Singapore
129809

John Wiley & Sons Canada Ltd, 22 Worcester Road, Etobicoke, Ontario, Canada M9W 1L1

Wiley also publishes its books in a variety of electronic formats. Some content that appears in
print may not be available in electronic books.

***British Library Cataloguing-in-Publication Data***

A catalogue record for this book is available from the British Library

ISBN 0-470-85039-6

Typeset in 11/14 pt Garamond by Mathematical Composition Setters Ltd, Salisbury, Wiltshire
Printed and bound in Great Britain by Biddles Ltd, Guildford and King's Lynn
This book is printed on acid-free paper responsibly manufactured from sustainable forestry in
which at least two trees are planted for each one used for paper production.

# Contents

# Introduction

The British Psychological Society defines a psychometric test as: *an instrument designed to produce a quantitive assessment of some psychological attribute or attributes*. A meaning of the word metric is *measure*, and psycho means *mind*.

Psychometric tests are basically tools for measuring the mind and are used frequently by employers, as part of their selection process, because they believe that such tests assist them considerably in providing an accurate assessment of whether an individual is able to do the required job and whether the person's character is suited to the work.

Psychometric tests have existed since the turn of the nineteenth century, although attempts to measure the differences between the psychological characteristics of individuals can be traced back to Hippocrates at around 400 BC, who attempted to define four basic temperament types as optimistic, depressed, irritable and sluggish.

In the last 25–30 years, psychometric tests have been brought into widespread use in industry because of the need by employers to ensure that they place the right people in the right job from the outset. One of the main reasons for this in today's competitive world of tight purse strings, cost-cutting and low budgets is the high cost of errors, including the need to readvertise and reinterview new applicants, and reinvest in training. There can also be serious difficulties involved in dispensing with the services of someone who has just been hired, especially if a contract has been signed. Furthermore, if a new recruit causes personality conflicts within a team or department this may lead to unrest between other members of staff with the result that the team may underperform.

Although an organisation will not found its entire decision on the basis of an individual's test results, the use of psychometric testing in selection is now well established, and can be used to provide objective information about different areas of a candidate's skills, for example, the extent of their knowledge, motivations, personality and potential.

The two main types of psychometric tests used are personality questionnaires and aptitude tests. Aptitude tests are designed to assess a person's abilities and personality questionnaires help to build up a profile of an individual's characteristics. It is important that such tests are evaluated in tandem with each other since it does not necessarily mean that if a person scores well on an aptitude test, then they will be suited to the job. While you may be good at doing something, you may dislike it intensely, and success in most tasks depends on your personal qualities and your attitude.

Personality refers to the patterns of thought, feeling and behaviour that are unique to every one of us, and these are the characteristics that distinguish us from other people. Our personality implies the predictability of how we are likely to act or react under different circumstances.

In reality, of course, nothing is that simple and our reactions to situations are never so predictable. In many ways the word personality defies a simple definition, so broad is its usage.

Although through the years theorists have emphasised different aspects of personality, and have disagreed about its development and effect on behaviour, it is accepted generally that heredity and development combine and interact to form our basic personality.

In addition to heredity, many psychologists believe that critical periods exist in personality development, and these periods are when we are most sensitive to a particular type of environmental event, for example, when we are developing our understanding of language and, how well our basic needs are met in infancy, which can leave a permanent mark on our personality.

Very loosely, therefore, a **personality test** is any device or instrument for assessing or evaluating personality.

Although personality questionnaires are usually referred to as tests, this can be misleading since they do not have pass or fail scores. They are designed to measure attitudes, habits and values, and are not usually timed. Sometimes these questionnaires are incorporated into the employer's application form and sometimes they are used during the second-stage procedure.

The personality tests in this book are designed to measure a range of aspects of your character and make-up in a fun, lighthearted and entertaining way. Although preparation or practice does not affect the outcome of this type of questionnaire, it is, nevertheless, helpful to familiarise yourself with typical questions and typical test structure, and it is always a useful, and often revealing, exercise to use these tests to analyse yourself from time to time, and also have fun analysing your friends and family.

There is no requirement to read through these tests first before attempting them, just the need to answer them intuitively, and without too much consideration. There is no right or wrong response.

Whenever you are faced with a personality questionnaire, it is necessary to answer the questions correctly. Any attempt to guess what you think is the correct answer, in other words the answer that you think your prospective employer wants to hear, is likely to be spotted when your answers are being analysed since tests often guard against such manipulation by posing the same question more than once, but in a different way. At all times, simply follow the instructions and be honest with your answers.

**Aptitude tests**, or as they are perhaps better known, cognitive, ability or intelligence tests, do not examine your general knowledge, but are designed to give an objective assessment of the candidate's abilities in a number of disciplines, for example in verbal understanding, numerical, logic, and spatial, or diagrammatic, reasoning skills. Unlike personality tests, aptitude tests are marked and may have a cut-off point above which you pass, and below which you fail or need to be assessed again. Intelligence tests, or intelligence quotient (IQ) tests are standardised after being given to many thousands of people and an average IQ (100) established. A score above or below this norm is used, according to a bell curve, to establish the subject's actual IQ rating.

While it is accepted that IQ is hereditary and remains constant throughout life, and, therefore, it is not possible to increase your actual IQ, it is possible to improve your performance on IQ tests by practising the many different types of question, and learning to recognise the recurring themes. The aptitude tests in the second part of this book are typical of the type and style of question you are likely to encounter in actual tests and will provide valuable practice for anyone who may have to take this type of test in the future.

Employers use aptitude tests to find out whether the candidate has the ability to fit the required vacancy and they can also be used to identify suitable jobs for people within an organisation. These tests can be helpful to both the employer and the candidate in identifying strengths and weaknesses, and thus help to find the job for which the person is most suited.

Psychometric testing is likely to become even more popular and widely used by employers in the future. In the United States, The Graduate Record Examination for graduate entry into universities is being replaced over the next few years by a Computer Adaptive Test, which is an interactive form of testing where the questions are set in relation to the ease with which questions have been answered.

The latest trend in psychometric testing is ever more towards online testing. This will enable, or even require, candidates to complete and submit their test in advance of being short listed, thus enabling the employer to have the results in advance of the interview. Candidates will have ample opportunity to practise on similar tests in the coming months and years as sample tests proliferate on the Internet.

# Section 1
# Personality tests

# Part one

## Introduction

Part One consists of 20 tests designed to assess different aspects of your personality, including your creative and perceptual skills.

There are three different types of questionnaires in the first 18 of these tests, as shown below. In each of these you are presented with a statement or question relating to some aspect of your personality and are asked to respond to it in one of several ways according to the instructions given at the start of each test:

1   Respond on a scale of 1–5, with 5 being the most applicable to yourself, down to 1 being most untrue.

2   Answer a question or statement by choosing which one of the three alternative responses given is most applicable to yourself.

3   Rank four statements in a group according to which is most true to your character down to which is most unlike your character.

The procedure for completing each of these is to answer the questions as truthfully and realistically as possible, in other words, be true to yourself at all times in order to obtain the most accurate assessment.

There are no right or wrong answers and there is no time limit for completing the tests.

# How well do you cope under pressure?

1  How important to you is the need to succeed?

   a)  quite important
   b)  very important
   c)  it is not something I think about a great deal

2  How often have you taken time off work due to stress?

   a)  twice or less
   b)  more than twice
   c)  never

3  Do you believe you are a person who is thought of by others as someone who is able to keep a cool head in a crisis?

   a)  sometimes, but often someone who keeps a cool head in a crisis has not got a grasp of the situation
   b)  not really
   c)  yes, that is how I believe others rightly perceive me

4  Which of the following would you say would be most beneficial to reducing stress and enabling you to relax after a particularly busy day at the office?

   a)  a couple of hours sleep in my favourite armchair
   b)  a nice stiff whisky or other spirit
   c)  eat a bar of chocolate

5  Does working to deadlines give you a buzz?

   a)  no, but working to deadlines is a necessary evil most of us have to cope with
   b)  no, I find working to deadlines quite a worry and much prefer being able to set my own pace
   c)  yes, I believe I work well under pressure

6  Do you believe that modern living creates much more pressure than, say, 40 years ago?

   a)  perhaps
   b)  yes
   c)  no

7  You are suddenly asked to look after your nephew's three unruly children for the weekend due to a family crisis. How would you feel about doing this?

   a)  it would worry me
   b)  I would find the thought of it so horrendous that I would probably try to get out of doing it
   c)  I would relish the challenge

8  Have you ever damaged anything due to *feeling the pressure*?

   a)  not actually damaged anything although I have done such things as slamming down the phone on occasions
   b)  yes
   c)  no

9  Do you find that little, almost insignificant, things occasionally upset you?

   a)  yes, occasionally
   b)  more than occasionally
   c)  rarely or never

10  What do you feel about having to get to grips with new technology?

   a)   quite indifferent about it. If I have to get to grips with it because of my job, for example, then it is usually something I am able to cope with
   b)   it worries me somewhat
   c)   it is something I enjoy and find of interest

11  What do you think, for you, is the main purpose of weekends?

   a)   a time when I can spend more time with my friends and family
   b)   a time when I don't have to work quite as hard as I do the rest of the week, however, I am not in a position where I can completely switch off
   c)   a time for giving myself a mental and emotional break

12  When your house is being decorated, or when you are having other alterations carried out, how do you feel?

   a)   it does not bother me in particular as these things have to be done
   b)   somewhat on edge until it is completed, especially as it disturbs my routine
   c)   quite happy about it and sometimes quite excited depending upon what is being done

13  Do you have friends who you trust completely and can talk to in turbulent times?

   a)   maybe
   b)   not really
   c)   yes

14  Do you feel that more than ever we are living today in a competitive world?

a) I would say that the modern world is perhaps a little more competitive than a generation or so ago
b) yes, very much so
c) no more competitive than it ever was

15 Do you ever discuss your feelings with other people?

a) occasionally
b) rarely or never
c) more than occasionally

16 Do you believe in pushing yourself harder and harder?

a) sometimes
b) yes, that is the best way to make a success out of life
c) no, life's too short

17 How do you feel about having several tasks on the go at the same time?

a) it does not bother me
b) I prefer one job at a time
c) I prefer having several tasks on the go at the same time

18 How often do you get angry and upset with yourself if you make a mistake or things do not go the way you expected?

a) occasionally, as I suppose do most people
b) probably more than the average person
c) probably less than the average person

19 Have you ever taken any sort of medication, including pills, in order to relieve stress?

a) occasionally
b) more than occasionally
c) never

20  Has your own health ever suffered due to the death or illness of a loved one?

    a)  no, but maybe it would do in the future, I just do not know

    b)  yes

    c)  no, I have coped with, and have suffered, grief and upset, as have all of us, but my own health has never suffered as a result

21  Have you ever suffered from stress due to the pressure of taking examinations?

    a)  perhaps I find taking examinations a little stressful but no more than the average person

    b)  yes

    c)  no

22  What are your views on alternative therapy such as acupuncture in order to relieve stress?

    a)  not sure, perhaps it is something I might consider if the need arose

    b)  it is not something I would consider

    c)  it can be very beneficial

23  Do you ever get stressed out by the thought of doing small household chores such as washing up or cutting the lawn?

    a)  not stressed although such tasks can sometimes be something of an annoyance

    b)  yes

    c)  never

24  How easy is it for you to switch off completely, put everything completely out of your mind, and totally relax?

    a)  sometimes it is more difficult to switch off than at other times

b) it is almost, if not, impossible
c) I am in the fortunate position of finding it reasonably easy to switch off completely

25 How often have you felt the pressure of one thing and another is simply *doing your head in*?

a) occasionally
b) more often than I would like
c) rarely or never

26 You are sitting in a traffic jam. Which of the following is likely to be your strongest feeling?

a) anger
b) frustration
c) boredom

27 Do you feel more, or less, pressure the older you get?

a) about the same
b) more
c) less

28 What would be your feelings on removing to another house?

a) well, I quite like the house we live in now but perhaps a move at this time could have its advantages
b) an overwhelming task to be avoided if at all possible
c) a lot of hard work, but generally something to plan for, and look forward to

29 How often has your sex life ever suffered due to stress or pressure of work?

a) on no more than a couple of occasions

b)   more than a couple of occasions

c)   never

30  Have you ever suffered from stress due to having to give up something such as caffeine or nicotine?

a)   not apart from a few withdrawal symptoms

b)   yes

c)   no

# Analysis

All of us experience different degrees of pressure and stress at some time in our lives but we deal with it in different ways.

Some causes of stress are perhaps easier to deal with than others. The taking of school examinations, for example, is a common cause of stress. However, because we know for a number of years in advance that these exams will take place we have time to prepare ourselves both mentally and by taking mock examinations and revising.

The real examinations of life are, however, not so predictable. The following is a list of some common events and experiences which can cause stress. It is when these events occur unexpectedly and simultaneously (the double or triple whammy) that we are at our most vulnerable to stress.

Death of a partner
Divorce/separation/break up of a relationship
Death of a close relative or friend
Personal illness
Illness of a loved one
Moving house
Redundancy
Large mortgage/debts

Children leaving home
Changes at work – new job, boss, responsibilities

Common responses to stress include loss of sleep, irritability, short temper, worry and stress-related ailments.

Dealing with responses to stress can be difficult since what one person finds stressful or pressurising, another may not, and we all react to different stressful situations in different ways.

Nevertheless, a good starting point is increasing your awareness of the main causes of pressure and stress since this at the very least could help you in trying to see what you can do about it.

There are several suggested steps that you can take to combat stress or the effects of pressure.

Sometimes, the best cure is prevention and an analysis of the type of situations that you have found pressurising in the past should enable you to look out for similar situations that may occur in the future, and to recognise any warning signs that you are about to enter into a similarly stressful period.

It is, of course, desirable to maintain some sort of exercise to keep yourself in good shape, especially in times of stress.

It is also desirable to try to get a good night's sleep, and, if possible, especially when you cannot sleep because of the number of negative thoughts racing through your head, confront the cause of the pressure by writing down the thoughts that are occurring to you and then attempting to analyse and evaluate them.

It is also necessary to talk to people about the pressures that you are experiencing. In other words, do not bottle things up inside you. Confide in a friend, partner or relative, even, if necessary, a professional counsellor. It may be that after talking things through in this way, your fears may be put into perspective and the pressures no longer feel so great.

When the pressure is work related it is necessary to discipline yourself to switch off from the situation that is causing the pressure. This may be achieved by reserving weekends for yourself and your family in order to give yourself an emotional and mental break. If this is not possible, then try to organise a longer break. If this does not seem possible due to the pressures and workload which have built up, then remember that no one is indispensible and that the most important thing is your health and mental well-being.

## Assessment

Award yourself 2 points for every 'c' answer, 1 point for every 'a', and 0 points for every 'b'.

### 45–60 points

Your score indicates that you cope with pressure extremely well. You are likely to be thought of by others as someone who is extremely laid back and almost totally relaxed, and you are able to keep things in proportion almost at all times.

The only word of caution about being in the fortunate position of having this temperament and attitude is that you should still be prepared for potentially pressurising situations which inevitably will occur. You should, in other words, have the ability to plan for pressures and build in a leeway for the unexpected.

It is also worth remembering that a certain amount of tension is positive since people do respond to, and are encouraged by, challenges.

### 31–44 points

While you do find yourself pressurised and stressed out on occasions, this tends to be the exception rather than the rule, and, more importantly, such situations are never long-lasting.

As a result, you are able to switch off somewhat where necessary and not push yourself too far.

You appear to be in the fortunate position of being able to look after yourself when you are facing pressure and you have the ability to say *no* if someone is making unreasonable demands.

## Less than 30

Your score indicates that you are affected by pressure in a negative way.

Since society's code of conduct prevents many of the natural ways to release pent-up emotions such as by violent means or by running away from the situation, pressure can, therefore, build up inside you and this is when you are at your most vulnerable to stress.

It is at these times that you may have a tendency to build things up in your own mind out of all proportion. However, it is worth remembering that most of the things that we worry about never happen, that most of the pressures which build up are short-term events and that if we deal with these pressures in a measured and structured way, then we should not be affected by them quite so badly. After all, these types of pressures are not restricted to just ourselves, they are the same pressures that are felt, at some time, by all people throughout the world.

You should also be conscious of the fact that pressure does lead to stress and many illnesses are stress related.

It is, therefore, essential that in pressurised situations you try to take one step back and reflect on your current situation, and your life in general and the positive things – there will be many – that exist and are occurring.

In general, try to develop a more positive attitude when dealing with what are termed modern-day pressures, but are, in fact, the same pressures which have always existed in some form for past generations. In fact, modern research should enable us to cope with these pressures better than we ever did in the past. At least now we recognise the danger of such situations.

Such a positive approach may include analysing and recognising the cause or causes of the pressure, your reactions to this pressure and your ways of coping with the pressure. It may also include changing your way of thinking about the pressure, improving the way you do things, for example, in a work situation, and knowing the best source of help and the right people to talk to when necessary.

It is also essential that you look after yourself when facing pressure, not just for your own well-being but for the benefit of those closest to you. This can be achieved in several ways, for example:

As well as doing the things that are absolutely necessary, do the fun things that you and those close to you most enjoy
Try not to be too self-critical, since we all make mistakes
Give yourself a break
Try to relax and sleep more
Keep yourself fit
Eat and drink sensibly
Cultivate other interests

# Are you a people person?

In each of the following, choose from a scale of 1–5 which of these statements you most agree with or is most applicable to yourself. Choose just one of the numbers 1–5 in each of the 36 statements. Choose 5 for most agree/most applicable, down to 1 for least agree/least applicable:

1 To get the best out of people you need to drive rather than support them

   5     4     3     2     1

2 I am not a very good listener

   5     4     3     2     1

3 I would prefer to go for a long walk on my own rather than in an organised group

   5     4     3     2     1

4 I do not have a great deal of patience when listening to other people's problems

   5     4     3     2     1

5 Winning is better than enjoying

   5     4     3     2     1

6  I do not suffer fools gladly

   5       4       3       2       1

7  I am much more comfortable talking to people on a one-to-one
   basis rather than in a group discussion

   5       4       3       2       1

8  I would describe myself as more determined than cheerful

   5       4       3       2       1

9  I am a great believer that people should stand on their own two
   feet

   5       4       3       2       1

10  I do not believe in giving money to beggars on the street

   5       4       3       2       1

11  There are things more important to me than success in my
    personal relationships

   5       4       3       2       1

12  I prefer to work alone rather than as part of a team

   5       4       3       2       1

13  I am more dominant than sociable

   5       4       3       2       1

14  I like to think of myself as something of a perfectionist

   5       4       3       2       1

15  I would describe myself as someone who keeps themselves to themselves rather than someone who goes out of their way to get to know people

5      4      3      2      1

16  I prefer to plan my own holiday than go on a pre-arranged group holiday with a set itinerary

5      4      3      2      1

17  I dislike social gatherings

5      4      3      2      1

18  I prefer individual sports rather than team sports

5      4      3      2      1

19  I need to be in control rather than going with the flow

5      4      3      2      1

20  I prefer to celebrate my birthday quietly and would not be very happy if someone threw a surprise party for me

5      4      3      2      1

21  I do not believe I would make a very good personnel officer

5      4      3      2      1

22  I rarely or never take part in charity fund-raising events

5      4      3      2      1

23  It does not worry me unduly that when I speak my mind it may upset people

5      4      3      2      1

24   I can often be intolerant of other people's views

     5        4        3        2        1

25   I do not tend to make friends easily

     5        4        3        2        1

26   I do not look forward to big social gatherings such as weddings

     5        4        3        2        1

27   I do not usually engage in conversations with strangers sitting next to me on long journeys

     5        4        3        2        1

28   People tend to view me as more of a loner than a mixer

     5        4        3        2        1

29   I do not often seek advice from other people

     5        4        3        2        1

30   I do not consider it important to put myself in the other person's shoes in order to see their point of view

     5        4        3        2        1

31   I am more tough than tolerant

     5        4        3        2        1

32   I do not generally feel sorry for the underdog

     5        4        3        2        1

33  If a work colleague won a million pounds on the lottery I would feel more envious than pleased for them

5     4     3     2     1

34  I am not interested in sitting on committees

5     4     3     2     1

35  It is important to get to know the right people

5     4     3     2     1

36  If someone telephoned me out of the blue asking me to sell raffle tickets for a charity I would probably decline

5     4     3     2     1

## Assessment

### Total score 130–180

Some people have a natural interest in all other people. They are, in effect, people persons, or people watchers. They take a keen interest in everyone about them, are curious to find out more about them and anxious to interact with them. Your score indicates that you are most certainly *not* one of those people.

You are what is sometimes, perhaps unkindly, referred to as a loner, or someone who likes to keep themselves to themselves, or stands somewhat aloof from others. While you do enjoy the company of others, this is usually restricted to a very close and exclusively small circle of family and friends.

This is fine just as long as it is what makes you happy and provides what you like out of life and does not frustrate your ambitions.

It is, however, worth remembering that no one can be an island entirely. We all depend to a certain extent on other people to make both our personal and business lives happy and successful. The more we interact with people both on a one-to-one and group basis, the happier and more successful all aspects of our lives will be. This does not necessarily have to involve going to all kinds of social gatherings and being the life and soul of the party. What it does involve is having empathy with others, having regard for their feelings and making an effort to get to know all others, irrespective of their class or status, and gaining their respect.

Keywords: disinterested, unsociable, withdrawn, diffident.

## Total score 91–129

Preoccupation with other people may not, to you, be one of life's most important priorities, nevertheless, you do tend to go somewhat out of your way to be fair to all people, and treat all people in an equal manner, and you recognise that basically all people are decent and that there is no reason not to get to know them better and behave in a polite and pleasant manner towards them.

As a result of this attitude you do tend to be liked and respected by others for what you are.

You prefer to treat others as you would wish them to treat you. A neighbour, for example, is someone with whom you like to exchange pleasantries, keep on the right side of and be there for in the event of an emergency. However, you would not go out of your way to find out their life history.

Keywords: adequate, tolerable, habitual, unbiased.

## Total score less than 90

You are most certainly a people person. You like observing people, assessing their personalities, finding out more about them and widening your circle of friends as much as possible.

In all aspects of your life you depend on other people to a great extent, in fact without other people your life would seem empty even to the extent of making you depressed and miserable.

You enjoy social gatherings immensely and find it easy to circulate at such events making small talk effortlessly when the occasion demands it.

The plus side of this is that you recognise the importance of the involvement of others in your life. You are, in effect, a good team player and appreciate the need to have the right people on your side if your life is going to be a successful one.

Your score also indicates a great deal of warmth of character, and someone who has a great deal of empathy with others, and this earns you the respect and trust of very many people.

The minus side is that some people may see you as being somewhat over-inquisitive, even intrusive. However, this is more likely to be the exception rather than the rule.

Keywords: empathetic, warm-hearted, concerned, regardful.

# Asking for what you want

In each of the following, rank the four statements in each group according to which is most applicable to yourself, which is least applicable, and which of the remaining two are next most applicable and next least applicable. Use the chart at the end of the test to tick your answers and work out your score.

1

a) I try to convey the right sort of body language whenever I ask for something

b) when I ask I need to be clear about my requirements and stick to my guns

c) if you wait until the time is right before asking you could be waiting for ever

d) I think it is important to wait until the time is right before asking

2

a) whenever I ask for something I plan my strategy carefully in advance

b) I am a great believer in the adage, 'ask and you shall get'

c) I never seem to be able to pluck up the courage to ask for what I want

d) whenever I ask for something I find that emphasis on humour is much more effective than boastfulness

3

   a) I always give my potential date an escape route when asking them out, in order not to embarrass them

   b) I never seem to be able to ask anyone out for a date because I simply can never pluck up the courage

   c) I never seem to be able to ask people out on a date because of the fear of personal rejection

   d) when asking someone out for a date it is important to find out their likes and dislikes in advance

4

   a) whenever asking for something face to face it is important to maintain eye contact

   b) when asking for something or complaining I always try to keep a smile on my face

   c) whenever I complain about something I fold my arms across my chest as this shows I mean business

   d) whenever I ask for something I try to remain unemotional at all times

5

   a) when really dissatisfied with the quality of a meal and the service in a restaurant, it is a good approach to say nothing at the time, but to write a polite letter of complaint to the restaurant manager afterwards

   b) the best approach when served with a meal in a restaurant which is not up to standard is to complain immediately to the chief cook direct

   c) if I get a meal in a restaurant which is not up to standard I usually end up eating it or leaving it rather than complaining and risking making a fuss

d)   if I am not satisfied with a restaurant meal I usually point this out to the waiter and ask if he can take this up with the kitchen staff in order to rectify the problem

6

a)   whenever I ask for something I try to keep my request as specific and straightforward as possible
b)   when asking for anything, *please* and *excuse me* are very effective phrases
c)   it is important to ask with authority
d)   empathy and sensitivity are very important when, for example, asking a friend to repay an overdue loan

## Analysis

There is an old adage which states: *you do not get anywhere in this world without asking* and another which refers to some people as *not being backward at coming forward.*

It is important, however, not just to know the best way of asking for something, but to know when is the best time to ask. Life is much more complicated than the simple philosophy of *ask and ye shall get.*

One of the most important things to consider when making a request is whether the time is right. For example, it is a bad time to ask a favour from your boss first thing on a Monday morning, or when he has come back from a couple of days' holiday and his desk is submerged in paperwork.

Having decided that the time is right, then phrasing of the request is all-important. A light-hearted, even humorous, remark in the first instance is helpful in creating the right atmosphere when, for example, asking for a pay rise so long as this is then backed up by valid reasons why you believe the rise should be granted. In effect, a request for a pay rise is the entering into of a negotiating process, and this is why preparation is so important prior to making any such request.

Having decided on your approach and requirements, it is essential to adopt the right attitude. It is important that you appear confident, but not cocky; relaxed and not tense; pleasant rather than confrontational; and business-like but unemotional.

It is also necessary to avoid antagonising the person you are approaching, and this also adds power to your elbow when making a complaint. You can still convey your request to the person to whom you are complaining without resorting to belligerence or being falsely apologetic. It is far better to state the complaint clearly and in a business-like way, and then go on to say what you think should be done about it.

At all times when making a request ensure that you are conveying the right body language. The folding of arms conveys the wrong sort of body language and can be seen as antagonistic, as does the pointing or wagging of fingers. Equally bad is over-smiling all the time, which can be seen as condescending. Far better to just maintain eye contact, which gives an air of confidence, but not over-confidence.

## Assessment

Scoring instructions (place a tick in the appropriate column for each letter):

| Group 1 | | Most | Next most | Next least | Least | Score |
|---|---|---|---|---|---|---|
| | a) | | | | | |
| | b) | | | | | |
| | c) | | | | | |
| | d) | | | | | |

| Group | Most | Next most | Next least | Least | Score |
|-------|------|-----------|------------|-------|-------|
| 2 | | | | | |
| a) | | | | | |
| b) | | | | | |
| c) | | | | | |
| d) | | | | | |
| | | | | | |
| 3 | | | | | |
| a) | | | | | |
| b) | | | | | |
| c) | | | | | |
| d) | | | | | |
| | | | | | |
| 4 | | | | | |
| a) | | | | | |
| b) | | | | | |
| c) | | | | | |
| d) | | | | | |
| | | | | | |
| 5 | | | | | |
| a) | | | | | |
| b) | | | | | |
| c) | | | | | |
| d) | | | | | |
| | | | | | |
| 6 | | | | | |
| a) | | | | | |
| b) | | | | | |
| c) | | | | | |
| d) | | | | | |

Award yourself 2 points for every 'a' answer ticked in *most*, 3 points for every 'a' answer ticked in *next most*, 1 point for every 'a' answer ticked in *next least* and 0 points for every 'a' answer ticked in *least*.

Award yourself 0 points for every 'b' answer ticked in *most*, 1 point for every 'b' answer ticked in *next most*, 3 points for every 'b' answer ticked in *next least* and 2 points for every 'b' answer ticked in *least*.

Award yourself 0 points for every 'c' answer ticked in *most*, 1 point for every 'c' answer ticked in *next most*, 2 points for every 'c' answer ticked in *next least* and 3 points for every 'c' answer ticked in *least*.

Award yourself 3 points for every 'd' answer ticked in *most*, 2 points for every 'd' answer ticked in *next most*, 1 point for every 'd' answer ticked in *next least* and 0 points for every 'd' answer ticked in *least*.

## 48–72 points

Your score indicates that you have the knack of knowing just how to ask for something and on the vast majority of occasions you are successful in your request.

## 24–47 points

While not scoring in the top range you still have the ability usually to ask the right question at the right time and on many occasions achieve the result you hoped for. You do, however, need to hone your skills even further and in this respect several of the suggestions made in the above analysis should prove useful.

## 23 points or less

Unfortunately, you need to work very hard on the skills necessary in asking what, for you, are decidedly awkward questions. In fact, it may be that on many occasions you have not been successful in getting what you wanted because you were afraid to even pluck up the courage to ask in the first place.

It is true, however, that on many occasions it is necessary to ask for what you want, whether it be to ask someone out on a date, ask your boss for a pay rise, complain about bad service in a restaurant, ask a workman to return and put something right that they have not done properly or ask a friend a favour. Such requests can usually only be successful if adequate thought is given to them. Sometimes it is a useful exercise to put yourself in the position of the person to whom you are making the request. For instance, how would you, in that position, best like to be approached and what attitude would you like the person making the request to adopt?

Keywords to bear in mind: planning, timing, phrasing, attitude, body language.

# Do you have the secret of success?

In each of the following, choose from a scale of 1−5 which of these statements you most agree with or is most applicable to yourself. Choose just one of the numbers 1−5 in each of the 35 statements. Choose 5 for most agree/most applicable, down to 1 for least agree/least applicable.

1  I am more of a doer than a thinker

   5       4       3       2       1

2  I am motivated more by my own inner beliefs and aspirations rather than the rewards they may bring

   5       4       3       2       1

3  In life you generally make your own luck, be it good or bad

   5       4       3       2       1

4  It is always too soon to quit

   5       4       3       2       1

5  I am a person who always puts in a great deal of hard work

   5       4       3       2       1

6 I am an extremely confident person

  5       4       3       2       1

7 I never abandon good intentions

  5       4       3       2       1

8 I can be ruthless when it comes to getting what I want

  5       4       3       2       1

9 I make people feel that being in my company is a rewarding experience, whatever their status in life

  5       4       3       2       1

10 Perfection is an impossible ideal

  5       4       3       2       1

11 It is important to give everything I do my best shot

  5       4       3       2       1

12 Success in life is much more than achieving your set goals

  5       4       3       2       1

13 I would be prepared to give up my favourite hobby, even though I love it dearly, if it meant success in my chosen career

  5       4       3       2       1

14 I am a very inquiring person

  5       4       3       2       1

15  I believe in grasping every opportunity that presents itself, even to the extent of taking chances

5      4      3      2      1

16  I find it easy to focus my mind on one subject for very long periods

5      4      3      2      1

17  I always look to the future

5      4      3      2      1

18  I am *not* a Jack of all trades, master of none person

5      4      3      2      1

19  I have no problem expressing my thoughts and feelings to others

5      4      3      2      1

20  Every day I feel I get mentally stronger

5      4      3      2      1

21  There is no such thing as a good loser, although some do show it more than others

5      4      3      2      1

22  I am not afraid of success, even though it may bring me enemies

5      4      3      2      1

23  Never give in

5      4      3      2      1

24  You do not become a success without the involvement of others

    5      4      3      2      1

25  When I am in the company of others I feel important and special

    5      4      3      2      1

26  It is possible for everyone to overcome social barriers

    5      4      3      2      1

27  I strongly believe that you must finish what you start

    5      4      3      2      1

28  I do not like to hear people boasting about their achievements

    5      4      3      2      1

29  I have far fewer worries than the average person

    5      4      3      2      1

30  I never do things by half-measures

    5      4      3      2      1

31  I am *not* nervous about making speeches to large audiences

    5      4      3      2      1

32  I am *not* afraid of failure

    5      4      3      2      1

33  Hard work is a means to an end

    5      4      3      2      1

34  I am clear as to where I see myself in 5 years' time

    5       4       3       2       1

35  I am a try, try and try again sort of person

    5       4       3       2       1

## Assessment

### *Total score 126–175*

It is sometimes said that the real secret of success is that there is no secret to success. It is certainly true that there is not just one secret of success, there are very many different factors which when combined together result in different levels of success for different individuals.

Your score indicates that if you are not already a success, then there should be very little doubt that you will be one day, and if you are already a success, then you will eventually reach even greater heights. You appear to have all the qualities necessary, such as character, persistence, flair and imagination, and not least the ambition to push yourself to the heights you know you are capable of achieving.

One word of caution is that you should take care not to become a total workaholic at the expense of yourself and your family, and, ultimately, your happiness. If you are able to succeed in striking the right balance, then you should be capable of reaching most of the goals you have set out to achieve in both your personal and working life.

### *Total score 90–125*

You do aspire to success and have many of the necessary qualities to achieve this, but perhaps you need to work a little harder at instilling some self-confidence into yourself to make you believe you can, and will, succeed. Perhaps success is something that you dream about but never really believe will happen. It is up to you to translate these dreams into reality and remove those self-doubts. You are a hard worker, but is this hard work done in the service of others and not for yourself? If so, try to develop the belief that hard work brings its rewards and that some of these rewards could and should be heading in your direction. Having convinced yourself, then it may be necessary to also convince others. This may not be quite as easy as it sounds, but it is certainly possible, as many have proved.

It is also useful to consider setting yourself goals. Many successful people set themselves goals which take them from where they are now to where they want to be. Such goals can be anything you want or need but when setting these goals it is also necessary to consider alternative goals, other people and other aspects of your life.

The advantage of forward planning is that you will then be clear in your mind what you really want. Having set the goals, then you need to take appropriate action towards achieving these goals, you need to monitor the results you are achieving, and you need to be sufficiently flexible to change, if necessary, what you are doing to achieve your goals.

## Total score less than 90

A great deal of hard work and commitment is required if you are going to make a success in a chosen career. But is this what you really want out of life? You may believe that happiness is more important in life than success. In fact, for many people happiness is success, and while happiness for many people is being a high-flyer, for others it is a stable family life, a steady job with not too much pressure and responsibility, and a regular income.

Also remember that there are different degrees of success. For many, success is holding down a regular and steady job for many years and doing that job well. For others, it is reaching the top of their chosen profession, and for yet others, success is nothing less than fame and fortune.

# How content are you?

1 Do you ever vent your own frustrations on other people?

   a)  occasionally
   b)  rarely or never
   c)  more than occasionally

2 How often do you wish you were someone else?

   a)  not often, but occasionally I have thought that some people
       are luckier than me to be who they are
   b)  it is something I have never seriously wished on myself
   c)  I have more than occasionally wished that I was someone else

3 Do you feel that you were born under a lucky star?

   a)  perhaps I have had slightly more than my share of luck in life
   b)  most definitely
   c)  no way

4 Do you ever feel you are stuck in a rut?

   a)  yes, from time to time
   b)  rarely or never
   c)  yes, I often feel frustrated that I am stuck in a rut

5 Do you feel that opportunities keep passing you by?

   a)  sometimes

b) rarely or never

c) regularly

6 If you could swap your lifestyle for a year, would you?

a) maybe in certain circumstances

b) I don't believe I ever would

c) yes, I would relish the opportunity

7 Do you envy the rich and famous?

a) occasionally

b) rarely or never

c) more than occasionally

8 Do you enjoy your job?

a) mostly, but not always

b) yes

c) generally, no

9 Do you often long for exotic holidays just to get away from it all?

a) yes, occasionally

b) holidays might be nice, but they are not a necessity in my life

c) yes, often

10 Would you ever consider plastic surgery to improve your appearance?

a) perhaps

b) no

c) yes

11 Do you feel that you make the most of your leisure time?

a) perhaps I do not have as many leisure activities as I would like

b) yes

c) no, because I do not have time for leisure activities

12  Do you usually get a good night's sleep?

a) I try to, but do not always succeed

b) yes

c) not usually

13  Are you envious of other people's possessions?

a) occasionally

b) rarely or never

c) more than occasionally

14  Do things ever weigh on your conscience?

a) yes, perhaps sometimes they do

b) rarely or never

c) yes, I am a worrier in that respect

15  How do you see the future?

a) with a certain degree of apprehension

b) hopefully things will carry on as they are now

c) I hope that the future will be much better than the past and present

16  Do you ever feel you have an inferiority complex?

a) maybe, on occasions

b) no

c) yes

17  Which of the following words do you think best sums you up?

a) balanced

b)   satisfied
c)   restless

18  Have you realised most of your ambitions so far in life?

a)   most of them
b)   I cannot think of any particular ambitions at the moment that need to be fulfilled
c)   not at all

19  Do you feel that you have a loving and stable family life?

a)   yes, on balance
b)   without a doubt
c)   not really

20  Do you have a light-hearted approach to life?

a)   yes, with most things. However, some things are too serious to be taken light-heartedly
b)   I do try to adopt a light-hearted approach to life in general
c)   I would not describe myself as a light-hearted person

21  Are you getting the most out of life?

a)   hopefully
b)   I believe that I am
c)   I do not believe that I am

22  How easy is it for you to sit back and relax?

a)   sometimes it is more difficult than at other times
b)   easily
c)   not at all easy

23  How often do you feel frustrated about wanting to do more?

a)   sometimes
b)   rarely or never
c)   almost all the time

24  If you were to step back and take stock of your life, which of the
    following would be most applicable?

a)   reasonably satisfied but still feeling that I could achieve much
     more
b)   I would count my blessings that I have had more ups than
     downs in my life .
c)   I would feel somewhat angry with myself that I have not
     made more of my life

25  Do you often feel pleased with yourself?

a)   occasionally
b)   more than occasionally
c)   rarely or never

## Assessment

Award yourself 2 points for every 'b' answer, 1 point for every 'a', and 0
points for every 'c'.

### 40–50 points

One definition of being content is satisfaction with the way things
are.

Your score indicates that you are content with your life. Therefore,
you are likely to have happiness and inner peace. It is this happiness
which rubs off on those around you, especially your immediate family.

Even if contentment in some people means that they lack the
ambition and drive of others, this is no reason to change their relaxed

attitude. If they are content, then there is no reason to change, since increased success does not necessarily bring with it increased happiness.

Remember the story of the man who was only happy when he was fishing. Fishing was all he ever thought about. He went fishing morning, noon and night and, as a result, he was always happy.

You are in the fortunate position of having found your own niche in life. You are happy and content with your lot, and that must be the envy of many people.

## 25–39 points

You are satisfied with your life, although perhaps you may not realise it as much as you ought to.

Although you do not lack ambition, you would never wish to pursue these ambitions at the risk of jeopardising not just your own happiness and settled lifestyle, but that of those nearest and dearest to you.

There is, however, often a feeling at the back of your mind that you could achieve more, and at times you find this a little frustrating.

Despite this, you do find that in general your aspirations have been fulfilled and there is, therefore, no real reason for change even if a host of other people such as friends, parents, teachers and co-workers are eager to tell you what you should do with your life. It is, after all, your life and these goals only matter when they matter to you, and you are, therefore, the foremost expert in defining which path your own life should take.

## Less than 25

Your score does indicate that you are in the main somewhat discontented with your life.

Perhaps you feel exasperated that you have not fulfilled your ambitions or yet realised your full potential. Maybe you think that life is all too short and that you have insufficient time to do all the things you always wanted to do. Perhaps you have a job that you really do not enjoy, and while you are at your place of work you are thinking of all the other things you could be doing that really interest and stimulate you, or perhaps you are just going through one of those difficult and stressful periods in your life that all of us, from time to time, experience.

If this is the case, then now might be a good time to step back and take stock of your life, and look especially at all the positive aspects. Ask yourself what you have achieved. Maybe you have a steady job and a stable family life – in themselves no mean achievement. Perhaps you have a sport or hobby that you enjoy, and could devote more time to. Any one of these is something to be thankful for, rather than a cause for despondency.

All in all, there are many things in our lives for which we can be thankful, and there is always someone worse off than ourselves. If you are able to focus on these positives, no matter how trivial or insignificant they may seem, then there is every chance that you will begin to find the inner peace and satisfaction that seems to have so eluded you in the past.

Although we should always try to plan for the future, we can only truly be happy right now. If you do enjoy the present and make the most of what you have now, then there is every chance that this will create in itself a much better future.

# Are you a control freak?

1  When shopping for yourself, do you prefer to shop alone or with your partner?

   a)  I prefer to be with my partner
   b)  no preference really
   c)  I prefer to shop alone when I am buying things for myself

2  Have you ever owned or wanted to own a dog?

   a)  no
   b)  yes
   c)  yes, I have a dog at present, and have had other dogs in the past

3  Do you believe the country would be a better place if you were in charge?

   a)  no
   b)  maybe
   c)  yes

4  The thought of which of the following would horrify you the most?

   a)  to be on an uninhabited desert island for five years
   b)  to spend five years in prison
   c)  to be a private in the army for five years compulsory national service

5 Do you prefer to be in charge of the television remote control?

   a)  no
   b)  not really. It is usually just left lying around for anyone to use
   c)  yes

6 You have just met someone in your former place of work which you left 12 months ago. Which of the following responses would most please you when you asked them how things were at the old place?

   a)  things are fine, everyone is very well
   b)  much the same, things do not get any better
   c)  things have never been as good since you left

7 Your usually submissive sex partner suddenly suggests that they take the lead in a bondage game. How would you react to this?

   a)  I would be very turned on by the suggestion
   b)  a little surprised, but would play along
   c)  quite taken aback and somewhat uneasy about the situation

8 You find that people suddenly start referring to you by your initials, for example, P.J. instead of Philip. How do you feel about this?

   a)  I can live with the situation, but would prefer them to use my correct name
   b)  don't mind in the slightest
   c)  rather pleased and flattered that perhaps my real name is surplus to requirements and recognition

9 Which of the following most closely resembles your own handwriting?

   a)  *t*

b)

c)

10  You and your partner, who are both able to drive, go out together in the same car. Who would you prefer to be driving?

    a)   my partner
    b)   don't mind as we are both equally good drivers
    c)   myself

11  Do you always let people finish what they are saying, or do you frequently find yourself interrupting them or finishing off their sentences for them?

    a)   I usually let them finish
    b)   I suppose that occasionally I may interrupt them or finish off for them what they are saying
    c)   I admit that I do frequently interrupt or finish off their sentences for them

12  Which of the following words best describes you?

    a)   dependent
    b)   average
    c)   important

13  Do you tend to sulk or play up if you don't get your own way?

    a)   I hope not
    b)   maybe, on occasions
    c)   I have to say that I do

14  If you miss a telephone call and call 1471 for the number, do you always phone that number back to see what the caller wanted?

a) not usually, unless it is someone I really want to speak to or they are returning my call
b) only occasionally, and then only if I recognise the number
c) yes, I almost always call the number back whether I recognise the number or not

15 Would you call yourself a faddish eater?

a) no
b) no, but others have called me a faddish eater on occasions
c) if that means having the will power to give up something I enjoy eating because it might not be organically good for me, then yes, I am a faddish eater

16 Are you interested in finding out as much as you can about all the people you know?

a) not particularly
b) not particularly, although I do join in the gossip from time to time
c) yes

17 Do you spend a lot of time on your appearance?

a) not really
b) not a lot of time, but I do take pride in my appearance
c) yes, the way I appear and the way people see me is very important to me

18 Have you ever played matchmaker?

a) never
b) once
c) more than once

19 Do you prefer to hold a dinner party or to be invited to one?

   a)   invited
   b)   no preference
   c)   hold

20  You are carefree and single and see someone you are very
    attracted to at a party. Which of the following would you prefer to
    happen before the end of the evening?

   a)   chat to them and eventually exchange phone numbers
   b)   ask them out for a date, or be asked out for a date in the near
        future
   c)   invite them to *your place or mine* that same evening

21  Do you believe in the old adage *if you want a job done, do it yourself*?

   a)   not really, that's too cynical for me
   b)   sometimes
   c)   usually, yes

22  Do you believe in pre-nuptial agreements?

   a)   no, it's a silly modern trend
   b)   only for the very rich and famous perhaps
   c)   yes

23  Do you ever feel stressed because you are not in control?

   a)   never or rarely
   b)   occasionally
   c)   more than occasionally

24  Do you want your partner to get to the top in his/her chosen
    vocation?

   a)   I only want for them what they would want for themselves

b)   I wouldn't push them, but if they do well for themselves I am pleased for them

c)   yes, I am keen for my partner to become successful in their chosen vocation

25   Are you generally satisfied with your *lot* in life?

a)   yes

b)   fairly satisfied

c)   no, I aspire for more

## Analysis

Control is something most of us long for in our lives, and many of us will go to great lengths to achieve it. However, some will go to much greater lengths than others.

There are many ways in which control-freakery can manifest itself, whether it is being fussy or over-fussy in the type of food we eat, controlling the way we look, even sometimes to the extent of undergoing plastic surgery, and planning ahead for all eventualities, by even, sometimes, making pre-nuptial agreements.

For many people, having more control, not just over their own lives but those around them, means they feel less stress, although this can have the reverse affect if and when it is brought home to them how little, in fact, they do control.

The following are a few of the tell-tale signs that you may be, or aspire to be, a control freak.

A desire for knowledge, especially about other people – knowledge is power
A desire to dominate others, especially your partner
Being very faddish about the food you eat, and having the self-control to maintain your strict eating habits
An enthusiasm to host dinner parties

You are something of a matchmaker
Extremely fussy about your appearance
A desire to control the spending habits of your partner

In general, the control freak has a need to be in control, and this also could mean a fear of not being in control. In extreme cases, this fear could manifest itself in the need to try and control people with sarcasm or even bullying

## Assessment

Award yourself 2 points for every 'c' answer, 1 point for every 'b', and 0 points for every 'a'.

### 36–50 points

Your score does suggest that you are to a certain degree a control freak.

While this may mean that you feel in control of your life and thus not so prone to stress as many others, it may be necessary to curb these tendencies somewhat before you become too obsessed with imposing your own desires, tastes and lifestyle on the world around you. In other words, before your desire to be in charge gets out of hand.

Although it is great to be in charge of our own lives, do remember that life is also a team game where we depend to a very great extent on the help, love, respect and friendship of others for our own happiness. We cannot expect the world to revolve around us. Therefore, it is necessary often to just go with the flow.

### 21–35 points

You are in the happy position of being neither a control freak, nor someone who is likely to be over-dominated by others.

It is likely that one of your chief priorities is to live in harmony with others and that you hold the belief that two heads are better than one, also that a problem shared is a problem halved, and that joint decisions are much more effective than those reached unilaterally.

## Less than 20

You are most certainly not a control freak, in fact just the reverse.

This means that in the main you are likely to have a relaxed attitude towards life in general and are happy to go with the flow.

The only problem is that you could be susceptible to being controlled, or even dominated by others. You should ensure, therefore, that your behaviour is not manipulated by others and remember at all times that you are your own person, and that the way you live and plan your life is ultimately your own decision.

# Forward looking, or stuck in a time warp?

1  Do you like to keep abreast of the latest technology?

   a)   not particularly
   b)   to a certain extent
   c)   yes

2  Do you constantly seek new hobbies and ventures?

   a)   not really, as any hobbies I have are things that I have been involved in, and have interested me, for many years
   b)   not particularly, although the occasional new interest may present itself to me
   c)   yes, I believe that every so often you just move on to new things

3  Do you go to new holiday places each year?

   a)   no, I usually go to the same place each year
   b)   not each year, since we have a few different favourite places that we like to alternate between
   c)   usually

4  Which of these is the most important to you?

   a)   the past
   b)   the present
   c)   the future

5 Do you tend to hoard things?

   a)  yes
   b)  perhaps
   c)  no

6 Which of these most closely represents your thoughts on 1 January?

   a)  here goes, another *annus horribilis*
   b)  it doesn't seem anything like 12 months since last 1 January
   c)  what new projects have I got planned for this year?

7 Do you believe there ever comes a time in life when you should just grow old gracefully?

   a)  yes
   b)  perhaps
   c)  no

8 Is there a particular era in the past where they played *your kind of music*?

   a)  most certainly
   b)  perhaps I do like music of a certain era better than today's stuff
   c)  no

9 Do you own a PC?

   a)  no, and I have no plans to
   b)  no, but I hope to own one in the future
   c)  yes

10 Would fond memories of living happily in the same home for many years prevent you from moving on to pastures new if you had the opportunity?

a)  yes
b)  it would depend very much on what the pastures new were
c)  no

11  Which of the following is most important to you?

a)  a content and stable family life
b)  live life to the full
c)  continually expand your mind to its full potential

12  When you spend an evening with your nearest and dearest would you prefer to reminisce, or plan for the future?

a)  reminisce
b)  both equally
c)  plan for the future

13  If someone does you a particularly bad turn, do you ever forgive them entirely?

a)  no
b)  not until I have evened the score with them
c)  forget them, rather than forgive

14  Do you have your own web page?

a)  no
b)  no, but I wouldn't rule out having one in the future
c)  yes

15  Have your idols/heroes remained the same through the years?

a)  yes
b)  yes, although I have some modern idols/heroes too
c)  no

16  Does the thought of new and seemingly complicated technology frighten you?

  a)  yes
  b)  more overwhelms and confuses me than frightens me
  c)  not frighten me, but sometimes I cannot rest until I have got to grips with it

17  Which of these most closely represents your attitude to change?

  a)  I hate change
  b)  I don't particularly like change but accept its inevitability
  c)  change does not worry me in the slightest

18  Do you prefer to watch repeats of vintage programmes on television rather than new programmes?

  a)  yes
  b)  sometimes
  c)  no

19  What do you think about new fashions in clothing?

  a)  not much
  b)  some new fashions are OK, I suppose
  c)  much of it is not for me but I like seeing people in new fashions providing it suits them

20  How easily are you able to move on from personal tragedy?

  a)  not at all easily, in fact it is a very long and difficult process
  b)  I try to move on in time, although no one fully recovers from a serious personal tragedy or bereavement
  c)  it is not easy. However, I do try to put it behind me and get on with the rest of my life as quickly as possible

21  Do you ever visit your old haunts to invoke happy memories and renew old acquaintances?

   a)   more than occasionally
   b)   occasionally
   c)   never or rarely

22  Which of the following do you consider to be your greatest strength?

   a)   organised
   b)   responsible
   c)   energetic

23  How do you feel about the company you work for constantly introducing all the latest technology?

   a)   somewhat apprehensive, since I feel much more comfortable with what I know
   b)   I realise it is necessary in today's world in order to remain competitive, but sometimes I worry that I will not be able to adapt to the new technology
   c)   I welcome it unreservedly as an exciting new challenge

24  Do you think your schooldays were the happiest days of your life?

   a)   yes
   b)   not particularly, although I do have some fond memories of my schooldays
   c)   no

25  Have you ever mastered an item of new technology to the extent that you have shown someone else how to use it?

   a)   no
   b)   occasionally
   c)   more than occasionally

## Assessment

Award yourself 2 points for every 'c' answer, 1 point for every 'b', and 0 points for every 'a'.

### 40–50 points

You would appear to be someone who is extremely forward looking and not in any way stuck in a time warp.

What this means is that you are likely to be continually looking forward to, and planning for, the future, whatever your age. Change for you is something that need not necessarily be a bad thing, in fact you are excited by the plans you are continually making and excited about some of the opportunities the future may bring.

You are also keenly interested in new technology and have a desire to be involved in any new developments that are taking place and not get left behind. Of course, technological change is now taking place at such a rapid rate that most of us are at least one step behind with the latest gadgets or innovations, so you should not feel frustrated if you suddenly discover that some latest development has escaped your attention, or that the computer you bought six months ago is suddenly no longer the most powerful model.

Your philosophy is that you should never go back, and that in life we should be continually moving forward irrespective of age.

### 25–39 points

Our past memories and experiences make us what we are today. It is these experiences that enable us to live for today and give us a foundation on which to build for the future.

While your score does indicate that you are forward looking and like to make plans for the future, and keep abreast with the latest technology, you are also fond of your memories and of times past.

You are in the happy position of not being afraid of change and the new challenges and new technology that change inevitably brings.

You remain optimistic for the future but at the same time somewhat nostalgic for times past.

## Less than 25

Oscar Wilde once said that there were two things in life that were certain: death and taxes. Had he been alive today we suspect he would have added a third – change.

Change has always been inevitable, but today changes in lifestyle, attitudes and technology mean that this change is taking place at an even greater rate than ever before.

We can either resist this change, in which case we tend to get stuck in a time warp, or we embrace change and move forward with it.

It would appear that you are quite resistant to change and not particularly interested in moving forward at the rate this change is occurring. The indications are also that you are not particularly interested in new technology, but this may be because you find the prospect of getting to grips with it somewhat overwhelming.

Because you tend to look back at what you considered the *better times* you are probably something of a sentimentalist. The time in your life that you look back on the most is likely to be a particular era when a change in your life occurred for the better.

If, however, you change your philosophy just a little and consider the good things that are happening right now, then this will give you more encouragement to look forward to the future with a more optimistic outlook. You may then find that the pattern will repeat itself, and in years to come you will look back on the current era with the same degree of sentimentality that you have now for times past.

Also remember that we, all of us, are never too old to learn. While technological advances are taking place at a rapid rate, in the majority of cases these technological advances are made for the purpose of enriching our lives, and we can either be part of this life-enriching process, or we can ignore it and not reap the benefits it provides.

# How soft-centred are you?

1 Which of the following most closely represents your opinion of St Valentine's Day?

   a) a day when people who are falling in love or dating buy each other cards and presents

   b) a romantic day when you always buy your loved one a card and a present

   c) a day when people make a quick buck selling cards, flowers and chocolates at inflated prices

2 Which of the following is your favourite type of music?

   a) anything as long as it is lively and has a beat

   b) romantic music, be it jazz, classical or pop

   c) anything so long as it is loud and brassy or stirring

3 After an argument with your partner, would you buy them a gift to make it up, even though you did not believe it was you that was at fault?

   a) maybe

   b) yes

   c) no way

4 If your work colleague was on a final warning for careless workmanship, would you take the blame for them to prevent them from being sacked after yet another error?

a)   it would all depend, perhaps so if they were also one of my close friends and/or they had a wife and family to support

b)   yes

c)   no

5   Do you feel sorry for beggars in the street?

a)   yes

b)   yes, and I often give them money

c)   no

6   Would you ever give a stray dog or cat a home?

a)   I think that I would if the situation ever arose

b)   yes, in fact it is something which I have done

c)   I very much doubt that I would

7   It is a very busy time at work and you are up to your eyes in important paperwork and a demanding schedule. Under those circumstances would you take a couple of days off to spend some much needed quality time with your partner?

a)   yes, but I wouldn't really be at ease with the thought of all that work on my mind, so under the circumstances it wouldn't really be quality time

b)   yes

c)   no, it would be irresponsible to leave my important work undone under the circumstances and I would hope that my partner would understand

8   Do you always tell your partner about any of their habits which you find annoying?

a)   occasionally

b)   never or very rarely

c)   more than occasionally

9  You have booked tickets to see your favourite pop star who you have been waiting to see live for years. Then a close friend asks you to help out at a charity event they have organised. You know that they have taken too much on and have no one else to turn to. What would you do?

   a)  tell your friend you will help them out if it is absolutely necessary but also explain about your plans to see the pop concert

   b)  help them out and cancel your visit to the pop concert, and not even tell your friend you had something else planned

   c)  under the circumstances, I could not miss the once-in-a-lifetime opportunity to see my favourite pop star

10  Your partner seems tired and preoccupied about something. How do you react?

   a)  say nothing immediately, but after a day or so, if they appear no better, ask them if they are feeling OK

   b)  tell them you are worried about them and ask if everything is OK

   c)  say nothing in the belief they will soon snap out of it

11  If you saw someone fall full length in a crowded street, how would you react?

   a)  watch to make sure they get up and walk on or that someone nearer than you goes to their assistance

   b)  I would instinctively run to their aid

   c)  probably do nothing but hope they are OK

12  Do you usually feel sorry for the underdog?

   a)  sometimes

   b)  usually

   c)  not particularly

13  Have you ever written someone a love-letter?

    a)  occasionally
    b)  more than occasionally
    c)  rarely or never

14  What would be your idea of the perfect romantic evening in with someone you were dating?

    a)  a meal, a sexy movie and some intimate passion for afters
    b)  a meal, comfortable sofa and a slushy movie
    c)  supper and breakfast

15  Do you often buy your partner presents?

    a)  not often, but I never forget birthdays and Christmas
    b)  yes, I like to surprise my partner with presents whenever I can
    c)  not as often as I should

16  Do you feel sorry for celebrities who are being vilified in the press?

    a)  occasionally
    b)  more than occasionally
    c)  never or rarely

17  How easy is it for you to say *no* when asked for a favour?

    a)  I have no problem if I feel the favour being asked is an impossible one or is unreasonable
    b)  difficult
    c)  not difficult

18  Late at night you turn on to the new channel and hear about a little dog trapped down a well, which a team of firemen are

trying to rescue. Which of the following would most apply to yourself the following morning?

a)   you would probably go about your usual routine, but might remember the story sometime during the day and mention it to a work colleague or acquaintance to see if they had heard whether or not it had been rescued

b)   the dog would be on your mind so much that you would tune into the news channel as soon as you got up, to try and find out if it had been rescued

c)   probably do nothing since you would have forgotten all about it

19   How often do you tell someone some home truths?

a)   occasionally
b)   never or rarely
c)   more than occasionally

20   Have you ever found tears streaming down your face when watching a sad movie or something sad on television?

a)   on rare occasions
b)   more than on rare occasions
c)   no

21   Have you ever cried with emotion because you felt so happy for someone other than yourself?

a)   only on very rare occasions
b)   more than on very rare occasions
c)   no

22   Which of the following qualities do you think is most essential for a successful long-term relationship?

a)   a good family life

    b) caring and sharing
    c) dynamic and continually stimulating

23 Which of the following represents your immediate reaction when first seeing breaking news footage on television of a heinous act of terrorism?

    a) feelings of anger and outrage at the perpetrators
    b) great sorrow for the innocent victims and their families
    c) a feeling of *there but for the grace of God go I*

24 Have you ever found tears streaming down your face as a result of the emotion of watching a movie, or something on television with a wonderfully happy ending?

    a) occasionally
    b) more than occasionally
    c) never

25 Do you believe your heart rules your head or your head rules your heart?

    a) both equally
    b) heart rules head
    c) head rules heart

## Assessment

Award yourself 2 points for every 'b' answer, 1 point for every 'a', and 0 points for every 'c'.

### 40–50 points

You are an extremely romantic and caring person and you are often deeply touched by the feelings of others, and affected by news bulletins highlighting the plight of others to the extent that you often feel guilty that you are not out there helping them in some way.

Because you are such a soft-centred and caring person this does mean that you are liked and respected by others. However, it also means that sometimes you may be taken advantage of, especially if you find it difficult, almost impossible, to say no.

Keywords: romantic, caring, soft-hearted, idealistic.

## 25–39 points

While you are generally a soft-centred person who would go to great lengths not to hurt other people's feelings, it may be that there is a need to peel off one or two layers before this soft centre is revealed.

The advantage of this is that you are still tough enough to realise your ambitions while retaining the loving and caring side of your personality.

Like a great many people, you are a real softy at heart.

Keywords: loving, empathetic, confident.

## Less than 25

While your score does indicate that you are more of a hard nut than someone who is soft-centred, it may be that way beneath this apparent hard exterior there lies something of a soft centre. It may be that this apparent hard exterior is, in fact, something of an act because you do not wish to be perceived as being soft, or display weakness.

At the same time, you cannot in any way be described as a romantic or sentimentalist. However, this does not stop you from having a long and loving relationship and secure family life, and people will respect you and take you for what you are, and admire your honesty.

While you do not lack honesty, it may be beneficial, not just for yourself, but for those around you, to always keep in mind the feelings of others and to try and empathise with them.

Keywords: pragmatic, dispassionate, taciturn.

# Attitude

In each of the following, choose from a scale of 1–5 which of these statements you most agree with or is most applicable to yourself. Choose just one of the numbers 1–5 in each of the 25 statements. Choose 5 for most agree/most applicable, down to 1 for least agree/least applicable.

1  I am proud of my nationality

   5     4     3     2     1

2  I would tell a shopkeeper if I noticed his/her shop was selling food beyond its sell-by date

   5     4     3     2     1

3  Parents should teach their children the difference between right and wrong from a very early age

   5     4     3     2     1

4  People are basically decent

   5     4     3     2     1

5  I continually look forward to, and plan for, the future

   5     4     3     2     1

6  I try not to react to different people in different ways no matter what their status or authority

5       4       3       2       1

7  The more knowledge and information we each have about the world and its people in general, the better and safer the world will become

5       4       3       2       1

8  I am extremely worried about the level of crime and violence in our society

5       4       3       2       1

9  I believe in the basic principle that *the customer is always right*

5       4       3       2       1

10  There are very few people I know that I would not trust

5       4       3       2       1

11  I forgive and forget as quickly as possible

5       4       3       2       1

12  I am always frank and candid about who I am and what I believe in

5       4       3       2       1

13  I channel all my energies into making a good job of what I am doing

5       4       3       2       1

14  I am happy when others like and respect me

5        4        3        2        1

15  I am angry when people or groups of people become stereotyped

5        4        3        2        1

16  I try to understand the other person's point of view

5        4        3        2        1

17  I do *not* tend to complain a lot

5        4        3        2        1

18  I am eager to please others

5        4        3        2        1

19  It is unusual for me to stand or walk with my hands in my pockets.

5        4        3        2        1

20  I am anxious to learn about the beliefs of other people

5        4        3        2        1

21  I strive to keep myself fit and in good shape

5        4        3        2        1

22  In general, we make our own luck

5        4        3        2        1

23  I smile more than most other people I know

5        4        3        2        1

24  I keep a tidy house and garden at all times

   5     4     3     2     1

25  On first meeting someone I make a conscious effort not to judge that person by his/her appearance

   5     4     3     2     1

## Analysis

Nobody is born with an attitude. Attitudes are formed in many different ways, for example, having direct experience with people and events and the influences in our lives, such as parents, with whom many people hold the same beliefs.

Our attitude is something that is noticed by other people more than ourselves. In many cases, a person's attitude is a natural attribute formed by that person's personality. It is, however, very wide ranging, and very difficult to define.

Originally, the term is derived from the Latin *aptitudo* meaning *fitness*, thus, rendering one fit to engage in the performance of a particular task.

Another definition of attitude is the explanation of the actions of a person owing to how that person feels about something, for example, consciously held beliefs or opinions and emotional feelings.

An individual's attitude can also change owing to changes in circumstances or stimuli, and these changes can either be positive, a better attitude, or negative, a worse attitude. Sometimes attempts at changing the attitude of an individual may work, or they may have the reverse effect in which the attitude is changed but in an opposite direction to that which was intended.

Social psychologists have identified several ways in which attitudes are used by individuals.

One of these ways is known as the *knowledge function* where attitudes are used to organise mentally all the knowledge we have amassed about the world, and the using of information in this way can help us to make more sense of the world.

Another is the *value-expressive function*, the function we are all perhaps most familiar with, which refers to the use of attitudes to express one's values. In this way, your attitudes will reveal to others who and what you are, and what you believe in.

The third basic way in which attitudes are used by individuals is called the *utilitarian/instrumental function* and this is the method by which we obtain rewards and avoid punishment.

Finally, there is the *ego-defensive function* whereby attitude is used to help defend self-image or ego. Someone, for example, who feels inadequate in the workplace may try to make someone else appear more inadequate or inferior as a way of shielding his own feelings of inadequacy from the scrutiny of others.

## Assessment

### *Total score 90–125*

You have a very good attitude to life in general. This means that you are not only positive, but enthusiastic about all the tasks you undertake.

This positive attitude is noticed by others, and will stand you in good stead both in your business and private life.

There is no need for change.

### *Total score 65–89*

While your score means you have in the main the right attitude, there may still be room for improvement.

Even though you do not have an attitude problem, far from it, it may be a useful exercise from time to time to carry out a self-analysis to consider not just your attitude to any tasks you perform, but also your attitude to others in our society and the wider world.

## Total score less than 65

Attitude is more and more important in modern living. When we go into a shop we expect the person behind the counter to be not only enthusiastic and knowledgeable about the product he is selling, but also to go out of his way to be helpful and to be anxious to please the customer.

The keyword here is enthusiasm, and it is this enthusiasm for living that the person with the right attitude will convey to others.

Your score indicates that in certain, but not necessarily all, respects you may have an attitude problem, and it may therefore be worth analysing your score on the individual questions within this test, especially where you have indicated a score of 3 or less. It is in these areas that perhaps your attitude needs to be considered and worked upon.

Since our attitudes are often formed by external influences, it may be worth considering whether such influences are present, and if these influences are negative, how can they be changed in order that your negative attitude can be reversed.

The more we understand about our own attitudes and beliefs, the more chance we have of changing our negative attitudes to more positive ones.

# Optimist or pessimist?

1 Do you ever worry, for the future generation, about what the world will be like in 50 years' time?

   a) more than occasionally
   b) very rarely or never
   c) occasionally

2 If you break a mirror how concerned are you that it will bring bad luck?

   a) quite concerned
   b) not concerned in the slightest
   c) slightly concerned

3 When you take part in any sort of contest, do you expect to win?

   a) not usually
   b) yes, I usually expect to win
   c) I like to win, but realise that I will sometimes come out second best

4 How often have you chased your losses at gambling?

   a) never
   b) more than once or twice
   c) perhaps once or twice

5  Do you believe that in life there is the ideal partner for everyone?

   a)   only in fairy stories
   b)   yes
   c)   some people, but not everyone

6  Do you consider that your cup of life is half full, or half empty?

   a)   half empty
   b)   half full
   c)   neither

7  How would you complete the saying: *If at first you don't succeed ...*

   a)   give up
   b)   try again
   c)   try, try and try again

8  Do you always feel that it will be possible to achieve your goals in life?

   a)   less than usually
   b)   yes
   c)   usually

9  Do you agree that every dog has its day?

   a)   disagree
   b)   strongly agree
   c)   partly agree

10  After an adversity, how quickly are you able to pick yourself up and dust yourself down?

   a)   not very quickly
   b)   almost immediately
   c)   fairly quickly

11 How often do you lose sleep through worrying?

  a) more than occasionally
  b) rarely or never
  c) occasionally

12 How confident are you usually that you have made the correct decision when faced with a choice?

  a) not at all confident
  b) usually fairly confident
  c) I worry about it a little perhaps

13 If you had a bad dose of flu would you see the doctor?

  a) probably
  b) no
  c) doubtful

14 Do you believe in keeping your aspirations low, so as to avoid disappointment?

  a) yes
  b) no
  c) sometimes

15 Do you feel secure financially?

  a) no
  b) yes
  c) most of the time

16 Do you believe that when one door closes another opens?

  a) no, life is not that simple
  b) yes
  c) sometimes

17  Do you believe that your friends will never let you down?

    a)  unfortunately, no
    b)  yes, usually
    c)  not sure

18  Is it your philosophy that there will always be calm after the storm, or storm after the calm?

    a)  storm after the calm
    b)  calm after the storm
    c)  both, as life is full of ups and downs

19  How long does it take you to count your blessings?

    a)  very quickly
    b)  I could almost go on for ever counting them
    c)  about the same time as most other people, I suppose

20  Which of these song titles/lines is most applicable to your general outlook on life?

    a)  *The other man's grass is always greener*
    b)  *Look for the silver lining*
    c)  *Somewhere over the rainbow, bluebirds fly*

21  Do you expect to live to a ripe old age?

    a)  not particularly
    b)  yes
    c)  I hope so

22  Do you believe your next big break is just around the corner?

    a)  big breaks don't just happen, they have to be created
    b)  yes
    c)  hopefully

23 Would you take out a large mortgage, confident you would be able to make the repayment?

a) I might, but it would worry me greatly
b) yes
c) yes, but it would worry me somewhat

24 Do you believe that bad news always comes in threes?

a) usually
b) if it does, then it is always balanced out when good news comes in threes
c) it does sometimes

25 Do you worry about flying?

a) usually
b) rarely or never
c) sometimes

26 Do you believe there is an afterlife?

a) no
b) yes
c) I hope there is, but I am not sure

27 When you buy a lottery ticket or scratch card, do you expect to win?

a) not really
b) yes, I wouldn't buy one otherwise
c) I am hopeful, but also realistic about my chances

28 Do you believe in the ultimate triumph of good over evil?

a) not really, especially in today's troubled world

b) yes, good will always triumph over evil, that is why we are all still here

c) not sure

29 If you were stranded on a desert island, how would you rate your chances of being rescued?

a) I would probably resign myself to never being rescued, but retain that slight glimmer of hope

b) I would know in my heart of hearts that one day I would be rescued

c) I would just hope for the best and try to survive in the meantime

30 How often have you applied to become a contestant on a quiz show with aspirations of winning *loads-a-money*?

a) never

b) more than occasionally

c) occasionally

## Assessment

Award yourself 2 points for every 'b' answer, 1 point for every 'c', and 0 points for every 'a'.

## *45–60 points*

You appear to be the eternal optimist with a wonderful outlook on life, the modern-day Mr Micawber who is always expecting something to turn up!

Not for you sleepless nights worrying about things that may never happen. Instead you tend to look on the bright side whatever happens and firmly believe that every cloud has a silver lining.

As long as you do not become naive about life's sometimes harsh realities, then you will remain cheerful, to a great extent carefree, and happy in the confident belief that you can get the best out of life, but at the same time being well prepared to accept the inevitable ups and downs.

## 27–44 points

Like most people in this world, you are a realist. You realise that life is a roller coaster, but roller coaster rides can be quite exciting and stimulating, and hopefully the high points will exceed the low points, and this is what really counts in the end.

Although you do not appear to be a pessimist, perhaps something to be learned from the eternal optimist is that we should not worry so much. Remember that most of the things that we do worry about in life never happen anyway, so why worry about them until they actually do happen?

## Less than 27

Although you might describe yourself as a realist, you appear to be a born pessimist.

While this does not make you a worse person, and you can still be successful and make many friends, it does mean that you are probably seen by others as a negative person, and that you suffer from a great deal of inner turmoil and unnecessary sleepless nights.

It may be that this is a way of creating your own defensive shield against the consequences of what the future may bring. If it turns out better than expected, then you will feel good, but if it turns out badly you will not feel let down, since you have already prepared yourself for the worst. In actual fact, having such a negative attitude does not make things any better or worse in the end, and in some cases worry about the future can lead to stress-related illness and make negative things happen which wouldn't otherwise.

What you must try to do is not make mountains out of molehills. Instead, try to put negative thoughts to the back of your mind. Try to think of the positive aspects of your life. If you can do this, and admittedly it is easier said than done, and may take a great deal of effort on your part, then you will start to reap the benefits, not just in your well-being and state of health, but by an improved outlook on life in general.

# Are you a good team player?

In each of the following, rank the four statements in each group according to which is most applicable to yourself, which is least applicable, and which of the remaining two are next most applicable and next least applicable. Use the chart at the end of the test to tick your answers and work out your score.

1

    a) in each team there should be someone in charge or overall control

    b) it is more important for team members to have their own defined areas of responsibility than to have someone in overall control

    c) the best team leaders create the conditions necessary to motivate their team

    d) the best team leaders have the charisma necessary to motivate their team

2

    a) a team can only be at its strongest when its purpose is in line with all its members' wants and needs

    b) a team is at its strongest when it is working well within itself

    c) a team is at its strongest when clear objectives are set

    d) a team is at its strongest when the objectives set may at first glance seem too difficult to achieve

3

a) I will channel all my energies into fulfilling all the needs and objectives of my team.
b) I am ambitious and will channel a great deal of my energies into becoming team leader
c) one of the greatest motivators is responding to a challenge
d) I aspire to be team leader

4

a) the best team leaders have the ability of helping others to see the best in themselves
b) the most effective team leaders are those who take a back seat as long as the team is working efficiently, and only become involved when something goes wrong
c) a good leader should encourage a feeling of camaraderie between the team members
d) a good leader is a catalyst for motivation

5

a) teams and team members are stimulated by being given responsibility
b) team members should be aware of the consequences of making errors
c) teams should never be afraid of making changes
d) team members should continually analyse and appraise each other

6

a) I believe the team will be better off as a result of my participation
b) team members should be equally adept at doing any job within the team

c) it is important I am there to assist all my fellow team members at all times

d) regular team meetings are essential in order to evaluate performance continually and reappraise goals

## Analysis

A key word in building a good team is motivation, and a key question to be asked is, 'What makes us do anything?'

There are several factors to be addressed when considering what will constitute a good team and who will make a good team member. Some of these factors can be summarised as follows.

### What is the purpose of the team?

Motivation could be lacking if the purpose of the team is not clearly defined and is not in line with the needs of some team members.

It is often said that a team is only as strong as its weakest link.

### Who will be my fellow team members?

Camaraderie is a key factor in building a successful team. It encourages openness, communication, fellowship and loyalty.

A team is at its most effective when its members are all pulling together in the same direction.

A team should be well balanced and bring together all the different kinds of human skills and technical expertise necessary in fulfilling a particular task.

### Will the work be something that is of particular interest to me?

Team members need to feel that the work is important and that the mission is clear. Their interest and motivation will diminish if the aims of the team are not in line with their own aspirations.

## What challenges does the team face?

People either respond to challenge in a positive way, or walk away from it. In general, a challenge has the effect of motivating a team and helps them to pull together and respond to the challenge. The greater the challenge, the greater the effort. Challenge, therefore, is in itself a motivator.

Even though difficulties will occur and from time to time some members' needs and attitudes will change, and there will be some changes in personnel, if the members of the team are working towards these common purposes, then motivation should be sustained over a long period.

## Assessment

Scoring instructions (place a tick in the appropriate column for each letter)

| Group | | Most | Next most | Next least | Least | Score |
|---|---|---|---|---|---|---|
| 1 | | | | | | |
| | a) | | | | | |
| | b) | | | | | |
| | c) | | | | | |
| | d) | | | | | |
| 2 | | | | | | |
| | a) | | | | | |
| | b) | | | | | |
| | c) | | | | | |
| | d) | | | | | |
| 3 | | | | | | |
| | a) | | | | | |
| | b) | | | | | |

| Group | Most | Next most | Next least | Least | Score |
|---|---|---|---|---|---|
| c) | | | | | |
| d) | | | | | |
| **4** | | | | | |
| a) | | | | | |
| b) | | | | | |
| c) | | | | | |
| d) | | | | | |
| **5** | | | | | |
| a) | | | | | |
| b) | | | | | |
| c) | | | | | |
| d) | | | | | |
| **6** | | | | | |
| a) | | | | | |
| b) | | | | | |
| c) | | | | | |
| d) | | | | | |

Award yourself 3 points for every 'a' answer ticked in *most*, 2 points for every 'a' answer ticked in *next most*, 1 point for every 'a' answer ticked in *next least* and 0 points for every 'a' answer ticked in *least*.

Award yourself 0 points for every 'b' answer ticked in *most*, 1 point for every 'b' answer ticked in *next most*, 2 points for every 'b' answer ticked in *next least* and 3 points for every 'b' answer ticked in *least*.

Award yourself 2 points for every 'c' answer ticked in *most*, 3 points for every 'c' answer ticked in *next most*, 1 point for every 'c' answer ticked in *next least* and 0 points for every 'c' answer ticked in *least*.

Award yourself 0 points for every 'd' answer ticked in *most*, 1 point for every 'd' answer ticked in *next most*, 3 points for every 'd' answer ticked in *next least* and 2 points for every 'd' answer ticked in *least*.

## 48–72 points

Not only are you a good team player, but you have a clear understanding of what makes a good team player, and how to get the best out of a team, and as a result you should make a good team leader, if you are not one already.

A good leader is required to understand the importance of the team's purpose and challenges but also needs to focus on maintaining its camaraderie, responsibility and growth.

The best team leaders are able to create the right conditions in which the team is able to motivate itself.

If you are a team player, but not already a leader, then perhaps you should set your aspirations somewhat higher, but only if that is what you really want from life.

## 24–47 points

You are likely to prove a good team player with possible leadership qualities.

Both teams and individuals are stimulated by responsibility and you are likely to possess the right attitude to take these responsibilities seriously and to recognise the need for team members to pull together to achieve their objectives.

While a team does consist of individuals, it is only when these individuals pull together as a team towards a common goal that the team can really be effective.

## 23 points or less

It does appear that you are more of an individual than a team player, and as such prefer tasks where you are working on your own rather than as part of a team, and you also probably prefer taking part in an individual sport, rather than team games.

It may be that you do not like the interference of others, or that you do not like working under a team leader or captain, or that you are somewhat resentful of people who are put in charge when, perhaps, you feel you could do a better job, or perhaps you do not particularly like people in positions of authority.

Your score does, therefore, suggest that you will be most suited to a job or profession where you are allowed to work on your own, with as little interference and interaction from others as possible.

It should, however, always be borne in mind that life is to a great extent a team game, and that cooperation is always more productive than confrontation or isolationism. Team growth can also lead to individual growth in which we can all move forward by learning new concepts, increasing our skills, broadening our minds and sustaining motivation.

# How assertive are you?

1 You are a member of a committee and the position of chair suddenly becomes vacant. What is your reaction?

    a) I would be keen to fill the vacant position if I were asked
    b) I would do all possible to try and be elected to the vacant position
    c) I would consider standing for election to the vacant position but only if asked to do so

2 Do you believe that compromise is the best way to solve a problem?

    a) yes, but it must be a workable compromise that meets everyone's needs to some extent
    b) not if it means giving way to demands that are unreasonable, or that I strongly disagree with
    c) yes, since compromise is sometimes the only way forward

3 Which of the following is most important to you?

    a) the right to live in peace and harmony
    b) the right to say no
    c) the right to be treated fairly at all times

4 Your new work colleague, who you have not had time to get to know very well, asks to borrow £50 to pay a bill because he has a

temporary cash-flow problem. How are you likely to handle this situation?

a)   explain tactfully that you do not lend money to work colleagues
b)   I would have no problem refusing his request
c)   I would probably agree just this once so as not to jeopardise my future working relationship with him

5   You are in a queue and someone pushes in front of you. How would you react?

a)   make a tutting noise, or some other reaction, to make them aware you are annoyed about it
b)   I would tell the person to get to the back of the queue
c)   I would feel annoyed but probably do nothing

6   Do you ever find yourself being easily manipulated?

a)   sometimes
b)   no
c)   yes

7   You are in a shop and on the way out realise you have been short-changed by a very small amount. What is your reaction?

a)   tell the assistant you have been short-changed but accept their reaction
b)   point out the mistake and insist on getting the correct change
c)   let it go since you feel that going back would be too much hassle

8   Which of the following is most important in your working environment?

a)   car parking facilities

b)  flexitime

c)  good canteen facilities

9  How confident would you be at expressing your viewpoint at a meeting even though you know a large majority of people present will not agree with you?

a)  not very confident but may pluck up the courage to put my viewpoint forward anyway

b)  relish the situation because I am very confident in my powers of persuasion

c)  not very confident and would probably keep my thoughts to myself under the circumstances

10  How do you usually react to criticism?

a)  dispute what they are saying

b)  assess the criticism and respond appropriately rather than react to it

c)  feel quite upset but accept that the person making the criticism is entitled to their opinion

11  What do you believe is most important to effective communication?

a)  speed of response

b)  keep it simple and keep it short

c)  be polite and courteous at all times

12  You see some young children walking across the bottom of your garden. How are you likely to react?

a)  say hello to them and make some remark such as, *Now what are you doing in my garden?* but in a friendly sort of way

b)  point out to them gently but firmly that they are on private property

c)  do nothing in the hope that it is just a one-off

13 You are in the non-smoking part of a restaurant and someone at the next table lights up a cigarette. Which of the following is most likely to be your reaction?

   a) point it out to the restaurant staff on the assumption that they will tell the person that they are in a non-smoking area
   b) point out to them very politely that this is a non-smoking part of the restaurant
   c) probably do nothing

14 Which of the following do you believe is the most important?

   a) be tough with the person you are dealing with, and tough with the issue
   b) be kind to people but tough with the issue
   c) to respect the other person's viewpoint

15 A workman comes to your house and charges what you believe to be a grossly excessive amount for just 15 minutes' work. Which of the following is most likely to be your reaction?

   a) say, *Are you sure, it seems a lot?* However, if they insist, pay up reluctantly and put the episode down to experience
   b) say that you do not feel able to pay what they have asked and tell them what you think would be a reasonable amount for the work carried out
   c) say nothing but make a mental note not to use that workman again

16 Your boss asks you to complete a project to a deadline you feel is unreasonable and impossible. How are you most likely to handle this situation?

   a) reluctantly accept the deadline knowing that you may be late in completing

    b)   try to convince your boss that you need more time in order to complete the project to the highest standard

    c)   burn the midnight oil in order to complete the project on time and impress your boss

17  With which of the following do you most agree?

    a)   a problem shared is a problem halved

    b)   ultimately, you must find the solutions to your own problems

    c)   most problems resolve themselves with time

18  Which of the following do you believe is most important in winning arguments?

    a)   to be able to give and take

    b)   to keep self-control

    c)   to know you are right

19  Which of the following is most applicable to you?

    a)   I let my opinions be known

    b)   I ask for what I want

    c)   I take into account the needs of others

20  Which of the following do you believe is the most effective way to start a sentence?

    a)   I feel ...

    b)   I suggest ...

    c)   I understand ...

21  Which of the following words is most applicable to yourself?

    a)   patient

    b)   persistent

    c)   dependable

22 You are asked to plan a social event, but then someone else starts to take over, which undermines the work you are doing. How are you likely to handle this situation?

a)   do nothing and put up with the situation
b)   politely make it clear that it is you who has been asked to organise the event
c)   suggest they take over the running of the event from yourself, if that's what they prefer

23 Which of the following words is most applicable to yourself?

a)   emphatic
b)   positive
c)   impetuous

24 Do you accept yourself for what you are?

a)   yes, as long as other people accept me
b)   yes, with all my imperfections
c)   not always

25 Which of the following do you believe to be the most effective in winning arguments?

a)   do not continually interrupt the other party
b)   stick to the point
c)   be prepared to compromise

## Analysis

One definition of assertiveness is the need to stand up for our own rights and aspirations in today's sometimes intimidating world.

It is necessary for us all to possess basic assertiveness skills in order to see us through the day, in order to maintain our self-esteem and to provide a shield by which to protect ourselves.

As a result of applying these basic skills, we will feel better about ourselves, will recognise what we want, have the ability to say what we want, be able to apply the correct degree of persistence, will not leave ourselves subject to manipulation by others and will have the ability to respond to criticism in an appropriate manner.

We will thus have the ability to take more responsibility for what happens in our lives and take more control of our lives by deciding what we require and keeping focused on what we want. At the same time, we will be able to enjoy what we have already achieved and celebrate our successes.

Assertiveness is also knowing our own rights as an individual. These include having the right to ask for what we want, having the right to ask for what we need, having the right to make choices and having the right to say *no*. It is also having the right to be our own person and accept ourselves for what we are, including our imperfections.

In order for assertiveness to be effective, it is necessary to hone our communication skills. This includes understanding exactly what we are asking for, since people will tend to treat us the way we ask to be treated. The most effective assertive communication is, therefore, based on respect for ourselves, and respect for others.

Self-respect means that how we handle situations affects our chances of success, and how we feel afterwards. It also means being in control and not about winning every argument. If we lose control, then it is almost certain that the argument is lost.

## Assessment

Award yourself 2 points for every 'b' answer, 1 point for every 'a', and 0 points for every 'c'.

## *40–50 points*

You come over as a very assertive person who knows their rights and is not afraid of knowing and saying what you want in any situation.

There is no doubt that you believe that you are your own ultimate judge and each person must ultimately come to terms with the challenges of living by learning to cope on their own.

This is fine just as long as you do not become too demanding a person and that you retain compassion for the troubles of others. Also, that you are capable of keeping you demands realistic.

You should also ensure that your reaction to criticism is an appropriate one. If you *react* to criticism, rather than responding to it, this is a sure-fire way of losing the argument.

Remember at all times that some ways of asserting your demands are much more effective than others, and that it is impossible to win every single argument. If you feel the need to persist, then stay calm at all times. It does not really matter how many times you hear the word *no* in an argument, you only need one *yes* for success. Often, the word *no* is merely a step on the way to hearing the word *yes*.

Remember that assertiveness skills do not win every time. However, assertive behaviour maintains one's self-respect and generally makes you feel better afterwards

## 25–39 points

Your score indicates that you have the perfect balance of assertiveness skills required to maintain your self-esteem, to know your rights, to have the confidence to ask for these rights and, as a result, to feel good about yourself.

Consequently you are able to adopt a positive attitude, be assertive when required, and generally feel happy about the way you have conducted yourself.

You also have the ability to recognise the importance, when the situation demands it, of finding a workable compromise that meets not just your aspirations, but also the aspirations of others.

## *Less than 25*

While you may know your rights, it appears you lack the necessary assertiveness not just to ask for these rights, or know how to ask in the most effective manner, but to say no.

It may be necessary to analyse your individual responses to the individual questions in this test in conjunction with the above analysis to try and find ways in which your basic assertiveness skills are not as effective as perhaps they should be.

Remember that there is never any harm in asking. You will not hear the word *yes* every time, but you will **never** hear the word *yes* if you do not ask in the first place.

Bear in mind always that assertiveness means taking control of your communication and the way to create successful communication is by the use of direct, clear language, keeping things short and simple, keeping to the point, setting the scene and using silence where appropriate. It also means working on your listening skills – there is nothing more infuriating than being interrupted when you are in the middle of making a point, and it means fully understanding what the other person is saying even if that means asking them to clarify things.

You should, therefore, at all times endeavour to create a good rapport with the other party and at all times strive to be kind to people even if you are tough with the issue.

# How patient are you?

1 Do you believe in the old adage, 'Everything comes to he who waits'?

   a) mostly, but occasionally it helps to push things along somewhat
   b) no way, the only thing certain to come to he who waits is death and taxes
   c) yes, this generally proves to be the case

2 What is likely to be the outcome if you sit down to do a crossword puzzle?

   a) usually complete all the answers that immediately spring to mind and after that give up
   b) it is very unlikely that I would ever even attempt a crossword puzzle
   c) usually stick at it until I have completed or almost completed it

3 Do you like to work on one long, or difficult, project until it is completed?

   a) if possible, but sometimes I like to break off to do other things in order to refresh my mind
   b) not really, I have a tendency to have a lot of uncompleted projects on the go at any one time
   c) yes, that is what I prefer

4 How good are you, or were you, at revising for examinations?

    a)   not very good, I really have/had to force myself to put my mind to the task

    b)   terrible, I would have obtained much better exam results if I had revised more

    c)   quite good

5 Which of the following would you prefer to be doing?

    a)   walking the dog

    b)   pottering about in the garden

    c)   painting and decorating

6 Which do you think you have most of, the Wisdom of Solomon or the Patience of Job?

    a)   both, or lack of both, equally

    b)   the Wisdom of Solomon

    c)   the Patience of Job

7 Which is your least favourite part of a visit to the supermarket?

    a)   going up and down the seemingly endless number of aisles

    b)   queuing at the checkout

    c)   I don't really have a least or favourite part of a visit to the supermarket

8 How many books do you read in an average year?

    a)   more than one but less than 5

    b)   one or less

    c)   five or more

9 Do you think people would be justified if they said you did not suffer fools gladly?

a)  justified to a certain extent, I suppose
b)  I guess that would be a fair comment
c)  no, I believe that would be a very unfair comment

10  You are passed over for promotion at work, unjustly you feel, but your boss tells you that immediately an opportunity arises you will be seriously considered for the next promotion. Would you be prepared to wait for the next opportunity, or start looking for another job with better prospects?

a)  probably carry on but with less commitment to the job
b)  no, I would start looking for another job immediately
c)  I would carry on and hope my boss was true to his word

11  What annoys you most?

a)  musak being played in your ear while waiting on the telephone to speak to someone
b)  children shouting and screaming in public places
c)  bad language in public places

12  Are you a good listener?

a)  only if I find what I am listening to very interesting
b)  generally, no
c)  generally, yes

13  If you had a pet do you think it would be well trained?

a)  I would probably just train it the basics as a matter of my duty as a dog owner
b)  not unless someone else trained it
c)  yes, I would really enjoy training it

14  You go to buy tickets for a theatrical or sporting event that you would really like to see, but find there is a two-hour queue for tickets. Which of the following is most likely to be your reaction?

a)   in very exceptional circumstances I might queue for two
     hours
b)   I would not queue and would miss the event as a result
c)   it wouldn't be a problem, I would queue for the two hours to
     get the tickets

15  Would you ever do a job that involved performing repetitive tasks
    all day long?

a)   only if I needed a job, and the money, very desperately
b)   no, I could not possibly do such a job under any
     circumstances
c)   yes, I could cope with such a job

16  How often do you lose your temper?

a)   just occasionally
b)   more than occasionally
c)   rarely or never

17  What worries you most about having to do jury duty?

a)   the time I would have to spend on it
b)   that I would be able to maintain my concentration
     throughout a long and complicated hearing
c)   that I would make the correct decision

18  Do you find it difficult to maintain your concentration when
    attending a lecture or training session?

a)   only when it is about something in which I am not
     particularly interested
b)   yes, I get bored and fidgety and my mind wanders onto other
     things
c)   no

19  Have you ever complained to someone that they are being too noisy?

    a)  no, but I have been on the verge of complaining several times
    b)  yes
    c)  no

20  Which of the following words best describes how you think people see you?

    a)  changeable
    b)  restless
    c)  steady

21  Do you think you would make a good driving instructor?

    a)  don't know
    b)  no
    c)  yes

22  What is your attitude when failing an examination?

    a)  disappointed, but may try again later
    b)  will probably move on and try something new
    c)  try harder next time

23  Are you an amber gambler?

    a)  sometimes
    b)  yes
    c)  not generally, since I believe that amber means stop

24  Do you think you could ever write a novel?

    a)  yes, but I'm not sure I would have the ability
    b)  no
    c)  yes, it is something I would really like to do, if I ever get the time

25  What do you think about people who queue all night for the
    New Year Sales or to watch their favourite player at Wimbledon?

    a)   if that's what they want to do, it's fine by me, but I cannot
         ever see me doing it
    b)   they amaze me, since it is something I could never do
    c)   good luck to them if that's what they want to do, and I
         wouldn't rule out the possibility of doing it myself sometime

## Assessment

Award yourself 2 points for every 'c' answer, 1 point for every 'a', and 0
points for every 'b'.

### 40–50 points

You are in the fortunate position of possessing oodles of patience.

Patience is more than just a virtue. To possess it is one of life's
great bonuses. It enables us to complete tasks, to tolerate the
shortcomings of others and to be able to wait for the right
opportunity to come along. It enables us to reach greater academic
heights, because we have the patience to study, concentrate and
revise, and in our personal life it enables us to work at, and persevere
with, relationships.

Just so long as you remember that everything does not necessarily
come to those who wait, and that sometimes it is necessary to make
things happen, you have a patience and temperament that must be
the envy of many of us who are not as fortunate to possess these
qualities to the same extent.

### 25–39 points

You are likely to possess a great deal of patience when it comes to
certain things, but not others. If you like doing a certain thing, then

you have patience in abundance. However, if the task is not something you enthuse about, then even if that task is a necessary one you may find difficulty getting round to doing it, or completing it once you have started.

It is necessary, therefore, to try and discipline yourself to completing such tasks, and for this purpose you might find it useful to make lists and realistic timetables and then strive to adhere to them.

It may be that you have a great deal of patience when it comes to completing practical tasks but not in dealing with people, or vice versa. Because there are so many different types of patience, a certain degree of self-analysis may prove useful, since before we can try to strengthen our weaknesses we must in the first instance be capable of recognising them.

## Less than 25

It does not appear that you possess a great deal of patience for many things, and unfortunately this is the way many of us are, it is simply part of our character.

One positive aspect of having this type of character is that you may be quite a dynamic person who makes a great deal happen in their life, and if something does not happen quickly you move on to try something else that you hope will achieve a quicker result. However, the negative aspects of impatience do considerably outweigh the positive aspects.

It may be useful for you to analyse your responses to each of the questions in this test and consider carefully, in particular, those responses where you have scored 0 points. It may be that you lack patience for only certain things or situations, and this is something that needs to be worked hard on.

You should find that this is well worth the effort, since having patience is, indeed, a virtue from which we can reap many rewards, not least that we will feel less stress in our lives, and less overwhelmed by many of the tasks we need to undertake. As a result, our general attitude, well-being and quality of life will be improved considerably.

# Would you make a good contestant on *Big Brother*?

In recent years there has been a rapid increase in fly-on-the-wall documentary series and quiz shows, for instance, *The Villa* and *Survival*. However, by far the most famous and popular of these is *Big Brother*, which has become almost a national institution in several countries throughout the world.

In *Big Brother*, up to 12 contestants are locked in a house together for several weeks, remote from newspapers and television and contact with their friends and families, and with very basic living facilities. Their every intimate movement is observed 24 hours a day by cameras placed strategically around the house, and they are given various tasks to perform by the programme's producers, the success or failure at which will determine their food budget for the following week.

In various series, contestants have been filmed arguing, apparently falling in and out of love, fighting, frolicking naked in hot tubs, making love, forming cliques and friendships, showering and undergoing every emotion from wild elation to deep despair.

Each week, each contestant must nominate two housemates they would like to see evicted from the house, and give their reasons for doing so. The housemates with the highest number of nominations are then *up for eviction*, which is put to a public vote, with the housemate receiving the most public votes having to leave the house.

The *Big Brother* series is a psychologist's delight. The housemates come from widely differing backgrounds and because, inevitably, their personalities are different, it is part of the programme's attraction observing how these personalities, whether it be cool and confident, down-to-earth, young, vulnerable and hypersensitive, charismatic or obsessive, will develop, how the contestants will react to the different situations they will face, and how they will interact with each other.

In the summer of 2002's UK *Big Brother*, for example, the programme's producers were successfully able to spice up the programme, to the delight of the viewers and the media, which resulted in higher tensions between the contestants and record viewing figures.

Even if you are not already a convert to the programme, the following test should give you some idea as to whether you could possibly make a successful *Big Brother* contestant.

In each of the following, choose from a scale of 1–5 which of these statements you most agree with or is most applicable to yourself. Choose just one of the numbers 1–5 in each of the 25 statements. Choose 5 for most agree/most applicable, down to 1 for least agree/least applicable.

1  I am very outgoing and extrovert

   5      4      3      2      1

2  I would go on *Big Brother* for the life-enriching experience rather than to try and win the money

   5      4      3      2      1

3  The thought of being isolated from the rest of the world for up to six weeks does not worry me.

   5      4      3      2      1

4  The thought of being seen nude on national television and in front of a world-wide Internet audience does not concern me.

   5      4      3      2      1

5  I believe that appearing on *Big Brother* could make me a stronger person both physically and mentally and lead to bigger and better things in my life

5        4        3        2        1

6  It is possible that I may form close relationships with some of the other contestants

5        4        3        2        1

7  I am in good enough shape physically to perform any of the strenuous tasks that *Big Brother* may set me

5        4        3        2        1

8  I am strong enough mentally to endure six weeks in the *Big Brother* house

5        4        3        2        1

9  I would stay the course for the whole six weeks if necessary, and would not 'want out' after a couple of weeks

5        4        3        2        1

10  I would find the task of voting people off one of my most difficult

5        4        3        2        1

11  I would have no problem accepting the discipline, rules and regulations of the *Big Brother* house

5        4        3        2        1

12  I am a leader rather than a follower

5        4        3        2        1

13  I make friends easily and quickly

    5     4     3     2     1

14  I am adaptable and can turn my hand to most things

    5     4     3     2     1

15  I have a good and broad sense of humour

    5     4     3     2     1

16  Even though I may miss my friends and family, it is a situation that I can cope with

    5     4     3     2     1

17  I am not embarrassed when sexual innuendoes start flying

    5     4     3     2     1

18  It would not worry me what the national press were saying about me while I was in the *Big Brother* house

    5     4     3     2     1

19  I never bear grudges

    5     4     3     2     1

20  I am not oversensitive

    5     4     3     2     1

21  I would welcome the experience of sleeping in a dormitory with a group of people I have only just met

    5     4     3     2     1

22 I would welcome the experience of a back-to-basics communal existence for up to six weeks without modern home comforts such as my own room, television and radio

5      4      3      2      1

23 I do not anticipate a problem adjusting back to normal living after my *Big Brother* experience is ended

5      4      3      2      1

24 I can accept that during my time in the *Big Brother* house I will have little or no privacy

5      4      3      2      1

25 I am able to contribute fully to all the household tasks necessary in the *Big Brother* house, such as cooking, budgeting, cleaning, etc.

5      4      3      2      1

## Assessment

### *Total score 90–125*

It appears you have the necessary credentials to become a *Big Brother* contestant.

You are obviously an extrovert who does not mind being the centre of attention and baring your soul, and everything else, to the nation.

If you did apply, and were successful, the rewards could be great providing you were able to accept that your life would become the centre of media attention and bad things would be written about you as well as good. Many *Big Brother* contestants have moved on to bigger and better things in their lives as a result of their appearance on *Big Brother* and have come out of their experience much stronger mentally than they were before the experience.

## Total score 65–89

It is doubtful that you could go through the *Big Brother* experience unscathed and emerge a stronger person as a result.

If you did take the plunge, then you could only be a successful contestant by being yourself. The spotlight on each of the contestants is intense. If they try to be someone different from what they are, then this will soon be spotted. Likewise, if they try to employ any underhand tactics, then they will soon be found out.

Contestants can only survive providing they are true to their own character. Then the other contestants and, more importantly, the viewing public will accept them for what they are. They will either like what they see, in which case they are in with a chance of becoming the outright winner, or dislike what they see, in which case they will soon be evicted.

In many ways, the *Big Brother* series mirrors life itself, if at times in a somewhat exaggerated way

## Total score less than 65

You will most certainly not make a successful *Big Brother* contestant. Don't even think about it!!

# Are you a career person?

1 Have you ever gone out of your way to make friends with those whom you consider to be *the right people*?

   a) no
   b) yes, it is important to know the right people if you want to get ahead in life
   c) sometimes, since it does help on occasions to know the right people

2 How frustrating is it for you to get passed over for promotion?

   a) not at all frustrating
   b) more than frustrating − it hurts!
   c) a little frustrating perhaps, but I soon get over it

3 How hard do you push yourself at work?

   a) no harder than I have to − life's too short
   b) very hard in order to achieve my ambitions
   c) perhaps a little harder than I should

4 Which of the following would give you most satisfaction?

   a) to be secure and happy in my chosen profession
   b) to be highly successful and get to the top in my chosen career
   c) to be highly regarded and respected as someone who is extremely good at their job

5  How important to you is success and recognition?

    a)   I would find success and recognition more satisfying than important

    b)   very important

    c)   quite important

6  Your company are opening a new office in a different part of the country and offer you the job of branch manager. Which of the following is likely to be your reaction, assuming you are settled and happy in your existing home?

    a)   I would be very reluctant to move

    b)   I would wish to move and expect that my family would be pleased for me and support me in my decision

    c)   I would talk it over with my family and reach a joint decision with them

7  Would you ever tell an untruth in order to gain promotion?

    a)   no

    b)   yes

    c)   maybe

8  How easy is it for you to switch off from work at weekends and holidays?

    a)   very easy

    b)   I never completely switch off from work at weekends and holidays

    c)   sometimes it is difficult to switch off completely

9  How often do you bring work home at night in order to meet a deadline?

    a)   rarely or never

b) more than occasionally
c) occasionally

10 How important is it to you that people in influential positions are aware of your qualifications and achievements?

a) not very important
b) extremely important
c) fairly important

11 Do you always like to know everything that is going on at your place of work?

a) no
b) yes
c) not everything, but I like to take an interest in the company in general

12 Do you believe that you should be at the top of your chosen career?

a) no, I will gladly leave that sort of pressure to others
b) yes
c) if not at the top, perhaps higher up the ladder than I am now

13 Do you feel you are an expert in your chosen field?

a) no
b) yes
c) there is much more I need to learn

14 Do you talk a great deal about your job to your friends and family?

a) no, I believe in switching off and not boring people about what I do for a living

b)  yes, I probably do

c)  I am not aware that I do

15  What do you believe is the main purpose of obtaining qualifications?

a)  it stretches and exercises the mind and makes you feel you have achieved something

b)  to obtain a good job and further one's career

c)  to have a good CV

16  Would you spend six months working abroad away from your family and friends if you had the opportunity?

a)  very unlikely

b)  yes

c)  probably

17  How important is it for you to keep on the right side of the right people?

a)  not particularly important

b)  very important

c)  I try to keep on the right side of everyone

18  Which of the following is the most important to you?

a)  to earn an honest living

b)  to be in a position of status

c)  to be respected by my work colleagues

19  Are you looking forward to the day when you can retire and live a life of leisure?

a)  yes indeed!

b)  not at all, I would probably never retire if I had the choice

c) it is not something I am eagerly looking forward to, but I hope to make the most of my retirement when it arrives

20 If you wake up one morning feeling particularly groggy and suspect you may be coming down with a dose of flu, which of the following would you be most likely to do?

a) I would probably telephone in sick and return to work when I was fit to do so
b) go to work and soldier on for as long as I could
c) it would be foolish to go to work in that condition, so I would probably take the day off and hope I would be fit for work the following day

21 How much time and thought do you give to the way you dress and present yourself for work?

a) it is not something I give a great deal of thought to
b) quite a bit, since my image at work is very important to me
c) as much as it needs to look as smart and presentable as the next person

22 When attending a job interview, which of the following do you believe is the most important?

a) to come over as someone who is intelligent and enthusiastic
b) to look good and have a quiet air of confidence
c) to be highly qualified and have a good CV

23 If you were made redundant suddenly and unexpectedly, which of the following is most likely to be your immediate reaction?

a) how on earth am I going to break the news to my family?
b) totally devastated that I will have to find another job and possibly start again on the bottom rung of the ladder
c) a feeling of shock and rejection

24  Which do you enjoy most, your job or your hobbies?

  a)  my hobbies
  b)  my job
  c)  both the same

25  Do you believe it is necessary to be crafty in order to climb the ladder of success?

  a)  if it is necessary, then it is not for me, since it is not in my nature to be crafty
  b)  most definitely
  c)  it may help on occasions

26  Would you cancel a holiday in order to meet an important deadline at work?

  a)  apart from perhaps doing it to save my job I cannot think of any circumstances when I would
  b)  yes, I would under certain circumstances consider it my duty to do so
  c)  I would be very reluctant indeed to do so

27  Would you put your social life on hold in order to further your career prospects?

  a)  no
  b)  yes
  c)  perhaps some but not all

28  Would you pay for an expensive and time-consuming training course if you thought it would further your career?

  a)  very unlikely
  b)  yes
  c)  perhaps

29 Would you take a pay cut if you thought that in the long run it would further your career?

   a) I would never take a pay cut on the chance that it would further my career
   b) yes, if I thought it would benefit me in the long term
   c) very unlikely

30 Could you be a *yes-man* to someone you despised if you thought it would further your career?

   a) no way!
   b) yes
   c) maybe, but it would be a very bitter pill to swallow

## Assessment

Award yourself 2 points for every 'b' answer, 1 point for every 'c', and 0 points for every 'a'.

### 45–60 points

Your score indicates that you are very much a career person, and that possibly your career is the most important thing in your life.

You will do everything in your power to ensure that you are successful in your chosen career. You see your career not just as your way of life, but as a gateway to creating wealth, and possibly prominence, for you and your family.

The difficulty of being so preoccupied with your own career is keeping a sense of priority in your life. Because of the amount of time and energy that is necessary to create a successful career, the danger is that the career person will become a total workaholic to the single-minded exclusion of everything else.

## 27–44 points

You are a career person, but not obsessively so.

While your career is important to you, it is not as important as your family values, and you believe that having close family ties brings with it the rewards of stability, happiness and long-term purpose in life, and this is what motivates you, more than your career.

You are also likely to cultivate other interests and use your leisure time effectively.

You are likely to be someone who takes pride in their job, and is quietly ambitious, so that if the opportunity presents itself for career advancement you will grasp it, but you are not continually and consciously seeking to advance your career, and career advancement is well down the scale of life's priorities.

For many people, being able to strike the right balance between the core values of career, family and contentment means that they are successfully able to reach most of the goals they have set out to achieve in both their personal and private lives.

## Less than 27

While your score indicates that you are not a career person, this does not mean that you are not, or will not be, successful in your chosen career.

With many people, their career is their source of identity, in other words, it is who they are. With you, this is not the case, and your job is merely a part of who you are, along with many other things.

What we are in life is often the result of what values motivate us. What may motivate you is happiness and fulfilment rather that career success. While many people see happiness and fulfilment as being a high-flyer, for you it may be a stable family life, a steady job with not too much responsibility and a regular income. None of us can really find happiness in becoming what we really do not want to be.

# How obsessive are you?

1 Do you ever worry over whether some small duty or task has been performed?

   a) very rarely
   b) occasionally
   c) more than occasionally

2 How important is it for you to keep up with the latest trends and fashions?

   a) not at all important, it is something I think about very little
   b) not very important, but it is something I like to be aware of
   c) very important

3 How often do you yourself clean your car?

   a) less than six times a year
   b) between six and 12 times a year
   c) more than 12 times a year

4 Which of the following words do you feel is most applicable to yourself most of the time?

   a) attentive
   b) busy
   c) preoccupied

5  Have you ever had a hobby which has interfered with your job?

   a)   no
   b)   no, since one of my hobbies is my job
   c)   yes

6  Would you ever stay away from people who were sick, in case you might catch what they have?

   a)   no, not unless I was prevented from going near them by someone medically qualified
   b)   no, not unless I was warned not to go near them
   c)   yes

7  Do you clean your house every time you know you are going to have a visitor?

   a)   not particularly
   b)   only if I know the house needs cleaning and it is a special visitor
   c)   yes, I tend to make sure the house is looking its best whoever is coming

8  Do you find yourself frequently falling in and out of love?

   a)   no
   b)   sometimes, but not frequently
   c)   yes

9  Are you subject to frequent mood swings?

   a)   no
   b)   sometimes, but not frequently
   c)   yes

10  How soon do you start packing for a holiday?

   a)   usually at the very last minute

b)   probably two or three days before
c)   up to a week before

11   How often do you look at your watch on average?

a)   less than five times a day
b)   between five and 10 times a day
c)   more than 10 times a day

12   Do you set the burglar alarm every time you leave the house and before you go to bed at night?

a)   I do not have a burglar alarm
b)   I usually set it every time I leave the house, but not when I go to bed at night
c)   yes

13   Do you take care to eat only what you think is good for you?

a)   no, I generally eat what I enjoy
b)   sometimes I will not eat something if I feel it had disagreed with me in the past
c)   yes, I do take care with what I eat

14   Do you worry about your appearance?

a)   not at all, people will have to take me as they find me
b)   not worry, but I like to take some degree of pride in my appearance
c)   yes, I do tend to worry about what others might think of my appearance

15   Has your hobby ever interfered with a relationship?

a)   no

b)   no, since I tend to share my interests with my nearest and dearest

c)   yes

16   How often do you take a gamble in any form, for example, such things as lottery tickets, horse racing or bingo?

a)   never or very rarely

b)   less than five times a week

c)   five times a week or more

17   How many television programmes are you hooked on, to the extent that you never miss a programme?

a)   less than three

b)   between three and five

c)   six or more

18   Have you ever kept newspaper cuttings, or photographs of a famous celebrity?

a)   no

b)   yes, photographs only, or cuttings only

c)   yes, both photographs and cuttings

19   Have you ever experienced stress and anxiety because you have missed an exercise workout?

a)   no, I don't work out on a regular basis

b)   no, but I do like to work out on a regular basis

c)   yes

20   How often do you clean your shoes?

a)   only when my partner tells me they need cleaning

b) only when I can see they need cleaning

c) every time I wear them

21 How often do you go on a spending spree for personal items such as clothes?

a) only when I am in specific need of something

b) just occasionally, when I feel the need to treat myself or cheer myself up

c) every time I get the opportunity

22 Do you save money on a regular basis?

a) no

b) no, but I put something aside for a rainy day when I can

c) yes, for peace of mind, security and for a rainy day

23 Does having tasks and jobs that are incomplete worry you?

a) no

b) yes, but only occasionally

c) yes, more than occasionally

24 Is there any part of your life that you would desperately like to give up, but find that you cannot?

a) no

b) not at the moment, but I have been in such situations in the past and have overcome them

c) yes

25 How often do you find yourself washing your hands even though they may not be dirty?

a) very rarely

b) only occasionally

c) more than occasionally

## Analysis

In its mildest form, an obsession is a preoccupation with some task or duty whereby you cannot rest until that task has been performed.

There are many such obsessions, as with, for example, the need to clean and polish your car almost daily, do the washing up immediately after every meal, or set off to work at precisely the same time every day.

There are also other obsessions with which most of us can identify and which we all experience from time to time. The very act of falling in love, for example, can be said to be a type of obsession.

In psychology, the definition of obsession is any idea that constantly invades one's thoughts. Many such obsessions can seem almost beyond one's will and even though we may be aware of them there seems to be very little we can do about them.

In its most extreme form, obsession is classed as an anxiety disorder. Such obsessions are repetitive thoughts, images, ideas and impulses that seem to make no sense to the person they are affecting, yet they are to that person a cause of much worry and stress. Sometimes it is difficult to recognise the symptoms of obsession. An example of this is the obsessive exerciser who may experience some, or all, of the following symptoms.

> each time they exercise they push themselves harder and harder
> they feel stressed if they miss a workout
> they would prefer to exercise than doing other things that they enjoy
> they need to force themselves to exercise even if they feel fatigued or unwell
> they worry that they will be out of condition if they miss a session
> exercising ceases to become fun
> they cannot relax if they miss out on a session

These symptoms are typical of many other forms of obsession, sometimes referred to as obsessive compulsive disorder (OCD).

## Assessment

Award yourself 2 points for every 'a' answer, 1 point for every 'b', and 0 points for every 'c'.

### 36–50 points

Your score indicates that you are no more obsessive than the average person.

You are no more prone to worry and stress than the rest of us, and are likely to have a relaxed attitude to life in general.

### 21–35 points

Although you are not an obsessive person, your score does indicate there may be areas in which you do feel anxiety and there may be some tasks that you feel the need to perform that are not, in reality, as important as you sometimes believe them to be.

So, although you have no cause for concern in general, it may be advantageous to analyse your responses to the individual questions in this test, and think about any areas where you have scored 0, to ensure there is no danger of any little obsessions creeping into your life.

### Less than 20

It does appear that in many ways you can be very obsessive.

Obsession does affect us in many ways. Sometimes it is merely obsession with finishing a particular task, in other cases it can be more serious.

Mildly obsessive people may find they are obsessed with different things at different times. What they are obsessed with one week may not be the same thing they are obsessed with doing the following week. However, more seriously obsessive people may find that it is just one type of obsession that dominates their lives on a permanent basis, as in the exercise example given in the analysis.

The first step to overcoming any obsession is to recognise that you are obsessed. Because of your score on this test it may, therefore, be beneficial to analyse your answers to the individual questions in the test, in particular, the questions where you have scored 0. It is in these areas that you may need to think about whether you are performing a certain task too much, and why, and whether these repetitive habits really should be so important to you.

# How laid back are you?

In each of the following, rank the four statements in each group according to which is most applicable to yourself, which is least applicable, and which of the remaining two are next most applicable and next least applicable. Use the chart at the end of the test to tick your answers and work out your score.

1

    a)   noise is not something which bothers me very much at all
    b)   noise does sometimes annoy me
    c)   noise aggravates me a great deal
    d)   I can usually put up with noise although I prefer peace and solitude

2

    a)   I do not have a job in which I feel pressurised in any way
    b)   I sometimes feel pressurised at work
    c)   my job involves a great deal of pressure and working to tight deadlines
    d)   although my job is a busy one I get through all my workload in my own good time

3

    a)   I feel that I have a very relaxed attitude to life in general
    b)   I sometimes feel that I need to relax more

c)   people frequently tell me that I should relax more
d)   I only feel completely relaxed at weekends and holidays

4

a)   I like to do things in my own time and at my own pace
b)   I prefer to live to a set routine
c)   I feel very much ruled by time
d)   I always make sure that I am never late for appointments

5

a)   I usually try to think before I speak
b)   I talk fairly fast but do not gesticulate
c)   I am a very fast talker and tend to gesticulate a lot
d)   I am not a fast talker but do gesticulate a little

6

a)   queues and traffic jams do not particularly bother me
b)   queues and traffic jams do annoy me
c)   I tend to get quite agitated in queues and traffic jams
d)   I try to avoid queues and traffic jams if possible because my time could be better spent

7

a)   anyone can make mistakes
b)   I cannot afford to make mistakes
c)   I get very angry with myself if I make a mistake
d)   I always try to analyse my mistakes to ensure I don't repeat them in the future

8

a)   I spend a lot of time relaxing by watching television

b) I usually don't just sit watching television because I like to be doing other things at the same time
c) I cannot usually sit down to watch television for long periods because I have too much to do
d) I like to plan ahead what I watch on television

9

a) I try not to criticise other people
b) I am sometimes critical of others
c) I am often critical of others
d) I tend not to criticise other people very much

10

a) life is only a game, and you win some − lose some
b) I always play to win
c) it is important to me that I am one of life's winners
d) winning is one of life's bonuses

## Assessment

Scoring instructions (place a tick in the appropriate column for each letter):

| Group | | Most | Next most | Next least | Least | Score |
|---|---|---|---|---|---|---|
| 1 | | | | | | |
| | a) | | | | | |
| | b) | | | | | |
| | c) | | | | | |
| | d) | | | | | |
| | | | | | | |
| 2 | | | | | | |
| | a) | | | | | |

| Group | | Most | Next most | Next least | Least | Score |
|---|---|---|---|---|---|---|
| | b) | | | | | |
| | c) | | | | | |
| | d) | | | | | |
| 3 | | | | | | |
| | a) | | | | | |
| | b) | | | | | |
| | c) | | | | | |
| | d) | | | | | |
| 4 | | | | | | |
| | a) | | | | | |
| | b) | | | | | |
| | c) | | | | | |
| | d) | | | | | |
| 5 | | | | | | |
| | a) | | | | | |
| | b) | | | | | |
| | c) | | | | | |
| | d) | | | | | |
| 6 | | | | | | |
| | a) | | | | | |
| | b) | | | | | |
| | c) | | | | | |
| | d) | | | | | |
| 7 | | | | | | |
| | a) | | | | | |
| | b) | | | | | |
| | c) | | | | | |
| | d) | | | | | |

| Group | Most | Next most | Next least | Least | Score |
|---|---|---|---|---|---|
| 8 | | | | | |
| a) | | | | | |
| b) | | | | | |
| c) | | | | | |
| d) | | | | | |
| 9 | | | | | |
| a) | | | | | |
| b) | | | | | |
| c) | | | | | |
| d) | | | | | |
| 10 | | | | | |
| a) | | | | | |
| b) | | | | | |
| c) | | | | | |
| d) | | | | | |

Award yourself 0 points for every 'a' answer ticked in *most*, 1 point for every 'a' answer ticked in *next most*, 2 points for every 'a' answer ticked in *next least* and 3 points for every 'a' answer ticked in least.

Award yourself 2 points for every 'b' answer ticked in *most*, 3 points for every 'b' answer ticked in *next most*, 1 point for every 'b' answer ticked in *next least* and 0 points for every 'b' answer ticked in *least*

Award yourself 3 points for every 'c' answer ticked in *most*, 2 points for every 'c' answer ticked in *next most*, 1 point for every 'c' answer ticked in *next least* and 0 points for every '0' answer ticked in *least*.

Award yourself 0 points for every 'd' answer ticked in *most*, 1 point for every 'd' answer ticked in *next most*, 3 points for every 'd' answer ticked in *next least* and 2 points for every 'd' answer ticked in *least*.

## 80–120 points

Your score indicates you are often on a very short fuse and quite intolerant of the many things that really annoy you. Because of your temperament, you find that many small things annoy you that do not particularly concern most other people.

Since this is in your nature, and likely to be the way you deal with things, it is easier said than done to relax more and try not to let things concern you so much.

This type of temperament manifests itself in many ways. You are likely to be very competitive, also quite ambitious, always in a hurry, rather impatient and easily irritated if things do not go your way, or things are not to your liking.

Although having a short fuse does mean that you have a release valve for your frustrations, it could have the effect of alienating many people towards you. It is also worth bearing in mind that anxiety does lead to stress and stress is the cause of many health problems, sometimes serious ones. So, if it is possible, try to discipline yourself to relax more and try on occasions not just to count to ten, but step back and reflect on your life a little more.

This may help you to get things into proportion so that when you do encounter those little things that irritate you, and which you often build up out of all proportion, you may do so with a much more relaxed attitude and outlook.

## 40–79 points

Although you do tend to find yourself stressed out and irritable from time to time, this tends to be more of the exception rather than the rule, and you are able to recognise the warning signs that you are pushing yourself too hard. You are, on these occasions, able to slow down, control your feelings, walk away from problems and push those little irritations to the back of your mind, realising that in the overall scheme of things they are of very little importance.

Even though you may be well motivated, and possibly quite ambitious, you are not dominated by work and its pressures.

## 39 points or less

You are in what many would call the fortunate position of having an extremely laid back and almost totally relaxed attitude to life. You are likely to be regarded by others as someone who is calm, casual, easy-going and patient. This does not necessarily mean that you are not ambitious, but it does mean that you prefer to work away quietly and unspectacularly towards your goal.

While you are in the happy position of being someone who is able to take life as it comes and in your stride, the only word of caution is that sometimes we need to inject a little passion into our lives and make things happen. The danger for some people is that they tend to be so laid back they almost fall over and are horizontal.

# Laterality

The meaning of the word lateral is of, or relating to, the side, away from the median axis.

In general, the term laterality can refer to any preference for one side of the body over another. Probably the most common example of this, and one to which we can all relate, is whether a person is left-handed or right-handed.

If we were to remove a brain from the skull we would see that it is made up of two almost identical hemispheres. These two hemispheres are connected by a bridge, or interface, of millions of nerve fibres called the corpus callosum which allows them to communicate with each other.

In order to work to its full potential, each of these hemispheres must be capable of analysing its own input first, only exchanging information with the other half, by means of the interface, when a considerable amount of processing has taken place.

Because both hemispheres are capable of working independently, human beings are able to process two streams of information at once. The brain then compares and integrates the information to obtain a broader and more in-depth understanding of the concept under examination.

In the early 1960s, the American psychologist Roger Sperry showed by a series of experiments, first using animals whose corpus callosum had been severed, and then on human patients whose corpus callosum had been severed in an attempt to cure epilepsy, that each of the two hemispheres has developed specialised functions and has its own private sensations, perceptions, ideas and thoughts, all separate from the opposite hemisphere.

As their experiments continued, Sperry, who won the 1981 Nobel Prize in medicine for his work in this area, and his team, were able to reveal much more about how the two hemispheres were specialised to perform different tasks.

For most people, the left side of the brain is analytical and functions in a sequential and logical fashion and is the side which controls language, academic studies and rationality. On the other hand, the right side is creative and intuitive and leads, for example, to the birth of ideas for works of art and music.

The following test is designed to discover whether you are basically a right-sided brain person or a left-sided brain person, or whether you are indeed in the fortunate position of having the right balance between the two brain hemispheres, and to identify the strengths and weaknesses of one-hemisphere domination.

1  Which of the following appeals to you most?

   a)  to be able to do things because I want to do them
   b)  to have a wonderful family life
   c)  to be highly successful in my chosen career

2  How strongly do you rely on your intuition?

   a)  very strongly
   b)  not very strongly, although I have occasionally followed my gut feelings
   c)  hardly ever, since I rely more on reason and logic

3  Which of these best describes you?

   a)  inquisitive
   b)  well organised
   c)  serious and studious

4 Which of the following most takes your breath away?

   a)  one of nature's great wonders such as the Grand Canyon
   b)  a great man-made structure such as the Taj Mahal
   c)  a great operatic voice such as Pavarotti or Domingo

5 How often do you worry about the way we treat our planet?

   a)  very often
   b)  occasionally
   c)  hardly ever

6 Which of the following do you most admire?

   a)  the flight of a bird
   b)  the speed and grace of a cheetah
   c)  the strength and courage of a lion

7 Do you like to set yourself targets and try to stick to them?

   a)  no, I prefer to do things when I feel ready and when I am in
       the right frame of mind
   b)  I do sometimes forward plan but in a flexible sort of way
   c)  yes, since that is the most efficient way to get something done

8 How important to you is punctuality?

   a)  not important
   b)  fairly important
   c)  very important

9 Which of the following do you find most difficult when sitting
   examinations?

   a)  concentrating and revising
   b)  conquering my nerves beforehand
   c)  worrying about whether I am going to score highly

10 Assuming you had time on your hands, which of the following would most appeal to you?

    a)   taking up something creative such as painting or sculpture
    b)   taking up a sport such as golf or bowls
    c)   joining a health club to keep myself in good shape

11 Which of these words best describes you?

    a)   complex
    b)   content
    c)   calculating

12 How often do you have dreams that you are unable to explain?

    a)   more than occasionally
    b)   occasionally
    c)   rarely or never

13 Which of these qualities best sums you up?

    a)   unconventional
    b)   wise
    c)   patient

14 How often do you doodle?

    a)   more than occasionally
    b)   occasionally
    c)   less than occasionally

15 Which of the following most irritates you?

    a)   rules and regulations
    b)   rudeness
    c)   incompetence

16  How often do you get flashes of inspiration or new ideas to the extent that your mind cannot rest until you have tried to put them into practice?

a)   more than occasionally
b)   occasionally
c)   rarely or never

17  Do you find it difficult to complete a long project or task without breaking off to do other things?

a)   yes
b)   occasionally
c)   not usually

18  What worries you most about retirement?

a)   nothing worries me about retirement
b)   perhaps getting older and not being as fit as I was
c)   that I may get bored and have difficulty filling my time

19  Which of the following most closely represents your views on making mistakes?

a)   making mistakes is all part of life's experience and it is important we learn from them
b)   the only people who do not make mistakes are people who do nothing, and that is the greatest mistake of all
c)   we all make mistakes but in life the winners make fewer mistakes than life's losers

20  Which of these words best describes you?

a)   philosophical
b)   peaceful
c)   pragmatic

21  What are your views on the old adage *so much to do and so little time to do it*?

   a)  I agree, and get quite frustrated about it at times
   b)  I accept that there are many more things I would like to do if I ever get the opportunity but it is not something that worries or frustrates me
   c)  it is not something that I give a great deal of thought to

22  Out of the following three choices which do you consider was your best subject at school?

   a)  practical subjects such as art or metalwork
   b)  sport
   c)  mathematics

23  Do you believe that aggressive behaviour is sometimes necessary as a means to an end?

   a)  not under any circumstances
   b)  maybe in certain very rare circumstances
   c)  yes

24  How would you best like to be described?

   a)  imaginative and innovative
   b)  amiable and well-liked
   c)  trustworthy and dependable

25  When making an important decision do you prefer to?

   a)  make your own decision
   b)  talk things over with someone close and reach a joint decision
   c)  seek advice from an expert

26  How organised are you when it comes to filing away important documents?

   a)   not well organised at all
   b)   reasonably well organised
   c)   extremely well organised

27  Which of the following words do you believe is most applicable to yourself?

   a)   visionary
   b)   steady
   c)   businesslike

28  Do you channel most of your energies into your chosen career?

   a)   no
   b)   I do take my career very seriously but have time to enjoy a great deal of other things besides
   c)   yes, I consider myself a specialist in my chosen career and it takes up a great deal of my time and energy

29  Which of the following best describes you?

   a)   emotional
   b)   decisive
   c)   aggressive

30  Which of the following would most influence your choice of a holiday destination?

   a)   beautiful scenery
   b)   sun, sea and sand
   c)   exciting night life

## Analysis

The right and left hemisphere functions can be summarised as follows:

| *Left hemisphere* | *Right hemisphere* |
|---|---|
| parsing | holistic |
| logic | intuition |
| conscious thought | subconscious thought |
| outer awareness | inner awareness |
| methods, rules | creativity |
| written language | insight |
| number skills | three-dimensional forms |
| reasoning | imagination |
| scientific skills | music, art |
| aggression | passive |
| sequential | simultaneous |
| verbal intelligence | practical intelligence |
| intellectual | sensuousness |
| analytical | synthetic |

The right-hand side of the brain controls the left-hand side of the body and vice versa.

While some individuals may be heavily weighted towards a particular hemisphere, this does not mean they are predominant in every one of this hemisphere's skills, since no one is entirely left- or right-brained.

The importance to each one of us of accessing both hemispheres of the brain is considerable. In order to support the whole brain function, logic and intuition, for example, are equally important. Generally, however, education systems in the western world tend, particularly since we live in a world of specialisation, to develop the analytical capacities of the left hemisphere at the expense of the creative talents of the right. Indeed, there was a time, not so long ago, when many schools would make left-handed pupils learn to write with their right hand, but thankfully this is no longer the case today.

## Assessment

Award yourself 2 points for every 'a' answer, 1 point for every 'b', and 0 points for every 'c'.

### *48–60 points*

This score indicates that you are a right-sided brain person. It is the right side of our brain which controls spatial ability, artistic expression, creative thought, inner awareness and, therefore, many of our subconscious thoughts and emotional reactions.

The right side is the intuitive hemisphere, which imagines and perceives things holistically. In other words, you like to see the big picture, rather than seeing the component details. As such, it is the side of the brain that reconstructs a whole pattern out of individual pieces, at the same time giving rise to our dreams, ideas and concepts.

It is also likely that as a right-brained person you have an appreciation of art and music. As a predominantly right-sided brain person you tend to learn in a subconscious and creative way, leading to an emotional reaction to situations as opposed to a measured and logical analysis. On many occasions it is possible that you have arrived at the correct answer to a question or problem without being sure how the answer was arrived at, and this is where intuition is so important to the right-sided brain person. Since the left side of the brain tends to process things in sequence as opposed to the right-brain approach, which is random, you may find that you have a tendency to move from one task to another before the first task is completed. This can often be a disadvantage, since you can find yourself with several different tasks all uncompleted. It may, therefore, assist if you can start making lists and schedules to discipline yourself to complete tasks more efficiently, and by setting yourself deadlines.

## 30–47 points

You would appear to have a good balance between the left and right hemispheres without being over-dominated by either side.

While this is a considerable advantage, it is, nevertheless, no cause for complacency.

One side-effect of hemispherical balance is that you could feel more conflict than someone with clearly established dominance. Occasionally, this conflict will be between what you feel and what you think and may involve how you tackle problems and interpret information.

On the positive side, the advantage of having a balanced brain is that with problem solving you can perceive the big picture and the essential details at the same time. An architect, for example, needs to balance creativity with logic and detail in order to turn a concept into a workable reality.

It is of considerable advantage to balanced-brain individuals that they have the natural ability to succeed in multiple fields due to the great flexibility of mind which they possess.

The learning and thinking process is likely to be enhanced when both sides of the brain work in a balanced manner.

## Less than 30 points

Like the vast majority of people in this world you are predominantly a left-sided brain dominated person.

The left side of the brained is analytical and functions in a sequential and rational fashion and is the side which controls language, academic studies and rationality.

The left-brained person will tend to process information from part to whole, that is, in a linear manner, as opposed to the right-sided brain person who likes always to be able to see the big picture first.

The left brain also tends to process things in sequence as opposed to a random order and the left-brained person is likely to be a fine accountant or planner. Also, spelling is likely to be a strong point of the left-brained person, since spelling involves sequencing. The left-sided brain person is also much more likely to be a specialist in their chosen field.

It may be advantageous to the predominantly left-brained person to employ certain right-brain strategies, in particular, the development of creative thinking skills and intuition. When attending a lecture, for example, a right-brained student may be at a disadvantage unless they have been given an overview of the whole concept first, since they essentially need to know exactly what they are doing and why. On the other hand, the left-brained student may not find it necessary to look this far ahead, but perhaps would find it helpful to do so.

# Creativity

The term creativity refers to mental processes that lead to solutions, ideas, concepts, artistic expression, theories or products that are unique and novel.

Because it is such a diverse subject in which there are so many different ways in which creativity manifests itself, and because in so many people it is to a great extent unexplored, creativity is very difficult to measure.

The French mathematicians Poincaré and Hadamard defined the following four stages of creativity:

*Preparation*:   the attempt to solve a problem by normal means

*Incubation*:   when you feel frustrated that the above methods have not worked and as a result you then move away to other things

*Illumination*:   the answer suddenly comes to you in a flash via your subconscious

*Verification*:   your reasoning powers take over as you analyse the answer which has come to you, and you assess its feasibility.

The creative functions are controlled by the right-hand hemisphere of the human brain. This is the side of the brain which is under-used by the majority of people, as opposed to the thought processes of the left-hand hemisphere which is characterised by order, sequence and logic.

Because it is under-used, much creative talent in many people remains untapped throughout life. Until we try, most of us never know what we can achieve, for example, one in three people in Britain have a desire to write a novel, yet only a very small percentage of these people progress any further than the initial stage of just thinking about it.

We all have a creative side to our brain, therefore we all have the potential to be creative. However, because of the pressures of modern living and the need for specialisation, many of us never have the time or opportunity, or indeed are given the encouragement, to explore our latent talents, even though most of us have sufficient ammunition to realise this potential in the form of data which has been fed into, collated and processed by the brain over many years.

Writers, indeed all artists, must use both halves of their brain. They must use the right side of the brain to create things and the left side of the brain to organise things. The creative and intuitive right side is able to cope with complexity and is where insights originate, while the left side controls language, academic studies and rational intellectual work.

The problem is, especially since in many people the left half of the brain is possessively dominant, getting these two halves of the brain to pass information back and forth and work together.

In order to perform any creative task it is necessary to encourage your right side to start its creative juices flowing, in other words, move your mental processes, albeit temporarily, from the dominant left side across to the creative right side. This may sound fine in theory, but not so easy to put into practice.

So, how can the predominantly left-sided brain person encourage the right side of his brain to be more creative?

Since such a person is so dominated by the left brain, one way is to lull your left brain into a degree of inactivity, or even bore it to sleep. This may, for example, occur on a long train journey or plane trip. At such times, your right brain has the opportunity to become more creative because it has less strong opposition from the fact-cluttered dominant left side. At such times, have a pocket tape recorder or jotter by your side and make a note of all the thoughts that occur to you no matter how strange, irrelevant or random they may seem. Most ideas, or insights, occur at random just for an instant. If you do not record them they are gone just as quickly, and probably lost forever.

At night, too, ideas come to us and our mind often behaves in a seemingly strange way. Again, this is because our logical and analytical left side is at its most inactive, and our subconscious right side is to the fore behaving in a mysterious and irrational way, giving rise to dreams and nightmares of which we often can make little sense.

Many writers keep notepads at their bedsides and force themselves to arouse from their half-sleep to jot these ideas, dreams and creative thoughts down.

In these periods of brain activity, do not pause to evaluate such ideas to decide which are of use and which are not. By doing so you will reawaken your dominant left side and will lose many of these thoughts before you have a chance to write them down. The evaluation of ideas is a left-brain activity and there will be plenty of time for that later.

So how does one put these new-found ideas into reality and start on the road to producing a first novel?

Again, there is the need to relax and put your left brain to sleep. This means no distractions. Most writers closet themselves away in seclusion since this is the only way they are able to create without interruption. Make sure the telephone is turned off, the study door is locked, you are fully relaxed and focused on the job in hand and have no negative thoughts about the task before you.

You are now ready to start. At first, just let the words flow at random for as long as they will. At this stage, there is still no need for any evaluation. Just keep writing without concerning yourself with spelling or grammar, or whether you are putting down exactly the right word.

At this stage, the object of the exercise is to get creative ideas on paper and expand on an original creative spark that occurred to you in a period of half-sleep, or boredom, during a long plane journey.

Then, when you have written all you can, begin to read it through, then re-read it and start adding bits to it and expanding on various parts. Again, ignore your left brain, since you are still seeking fresh ideas. At this stage, you are rewriting, adding and elaborating, and still generating new creative thoughts.

Finally, it is time for your left brain to be reawakened. There is now a need to organise what you have put down on paper. You accept it's something of a mess. The grammar is awful, so is the spelling, and it does not flow as it should. This is the least of your problems, and is the easiest thing to reorganise. It is what you are good at. Your left brain is now entirely in its element. The main thing is that you have created what you probably never even dreamed was possible – a work completely original to yourself from your own creative thoughts and insight.

Like many other tasks, or pleasures, the majority of us never know what we can achieve until we try. Having then tried, we instinctively know whether we find it enjoyable or whether we have a talent or flair for it. Then, if these signs are positive, we must persevere. By cultivating new leisure activities and pursuing new pastimes it is possible for each of us to exploit the potential and often vastly under-used parts of the human brain.

The following exercises, while different in themselves, are all designed with the object of improving or recognising your own powers of mental productivity, generation of ideas and artistic skill.

## Exercise 1

In each of the following boxes, use your imagination to create an original sketch or drawing of something recognisable incorporating the symbol already provided.

You have 30 minutes in which to complete the 12 drawings.

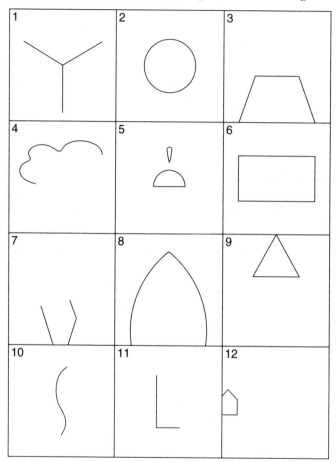

## Analysis

You can mark this test yourself, however, it is best marked by a friend or family member.

Award one mark for each recognisable sketch, providing it is not similar to any of the other sketches.

For example, if you draw a face, a second face scores no points since each sketch must have an original theme.

You thus obtain marks for variety. If you are creative you will tend to try to draw something different for each sketch.

There is no correct answer to each of the 12 sketches, since for each there are any number of ideas.

## Scoring:

| | |
|---|---|
| 11–12 points | exceedingly creative |
| 7–10 | very creative |
| 4–6 | average |

Repeat the exercise as many times as you wish. Try other geometric objects or lines as a starting point.

## Exercise 2

This test is based on Gestalt and Jackson's Test of Divergent Ability, which requires the subject to name as many new uses as possible for everyday objects such as a brick or a piece of string.

Here, you are required to name up to 12 new uses for a brick in 10 minutes. You should work strictly to the time limit, otherwise your score will be invalidated.

1 ..........................
2 ..........................
3 ..........................
4 ..........................
5 ..........................
6 ..........................
7 ..........................
8 ..........................
9 ..........................
10 ..........................
11 ..........................
12 ..........................

## Scoring and analysis

You can mark your efforts yourself, but it is better if you get a friend
or family member to do so.

Allow:
2 points for any good or original answer
1 point for a good attempt
0 points for completely impractical answers
0 points for any antisocial answers such as breaking someone's
window or hitting someone over the head.

Scoring:
18–24 points     highly creative
13–17 points     above average
 7–12 points     average

Now try the same again but this time think up uses for a 12-inch-
square piece of cardboard.

1 ...........................
2 ...........................
3 ...........................
4 ...........................
5 ...........................
6 ...........................
7 ...........................
8 ...........................
9 ...........................
10 ...........................
11 ...........................
12 ...........................

Now repeat the exercise as many times as you wish with other
common household objects such as a bucket, a comb, a rubber band,
a toothbrush or an empty milk bottle.

## Exercise 3

The object here is to interpret each of the 12 drawings below in the wildest and most imaginative way you can.

You may also try playing the game with other people. The main thing is to let your imagination run wild and lose you inhibitions. The more people laugh at your efforts, the more successful you are likely to have been in using your imagination and creativity. For example, you might think that drawing number 1 is a bulls-eye or target, but is there anything else it can be? Let your imagination run riot and see what you can come up with.

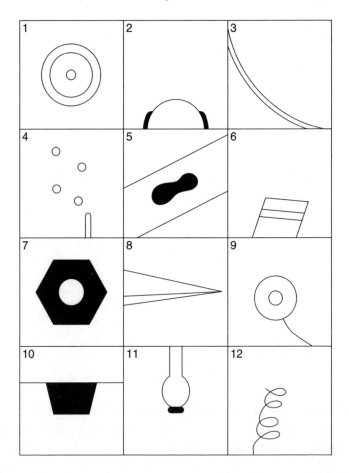

# Perception

In psychology, the term perception is so broad that it can embrace almost every aspect of the subject. In essence, it encompasses how we perceive ourselves, how we perceive others and how others perceive us. It also envelops how we perceive the world as a whole – the big picture – and how we perceive different events, scenarios and situations that occur within the big picture.

In order to perceive others sympathetically we need to have empathy with them, their character, aspirations and points of view.

Similarly, in order to fully understand ourselves we need to recognise and know ourselves for what we are, rather than what we would like to be.

One common cause of incorrect perception is the stereotyping of others. Because sometimes we fall into this trap, we tend to prejudge others on what we assume them to be like, even before we get to know them.

One of the most important aspects of perception is the ability to see more than one point of view.

The example shown below of the Necker cube consists of a simple line drawing:

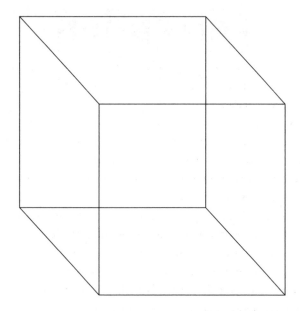

When you first look at the cube it appears quite unambiguous and
you are quite clear what you are looking at. If, however, you continue
to stare at the figure and keep your attention on it focused, then the
orientation suddenly shifts, then periodically changes back and forth
between these two orientations as you continue to focus. In other
words, it is a simple figure, yet our perception of it is continually
changing.

The Necker cube thus illustrates the importance of perception.
Two different viewpoints appear – yet, they are both correct. We
should, therefore, endeavour to see both viewpoints, and,
sometimes more specifically, both sides of an argument. This may
then enable us to reach a compromise, thus avoiding conflict. In the
very least, we should make an attempt to understand the second
viewpoint, even if that point of view is diametrically opposed to
our own.

The remainder of this chapter concentrates on just one aspect of
perception – *attention*.

In order to perceive any situation accurately, it must be focused on to the relative exclusion of other distractions. We must, in other words, give it our full and undivided attention and select from all that is occurring around us precisely what we need to focus on at that particular time and maintain our concentration and state of mental clarity on that situation.

One example of the difficulty in doing this is in a police investigation or court of law where a witness is asked to identify a person or describe an incident. On such occasions, it is commonplace for two genuinely well-intentioned and public-spirited individuals to give opposing versions of an event.

It is also possible to be misled into a false perception as, for example, in the question, 'How many times does the letter S appear in the name of the world's longest river?' Most people will start to count the number of S letters in the name Mississippi and overlook the fact that the world's longest river is the Nile. The correct answer to the question is, therefore, *none*.

The following test of 12 questions is designed to test your powers of perception and attention to detail, your alertness of mind and, in some cases, your ability to think laterally, and also your ability to avoid falling into the occasional trap that has been set.

In philosophy, perception is defined as the complex method of obtaining information about our surrounding world, specifically through our senses and adopting this information as beliefs. The problem with this is that our perceptions are not always reliable, since it is possible for us to misperceive what we believe to be correct and our senses are often susceptible to illusions. It is hoped to demonstrate in a number of the questions that follow that sometimes these fears are well founded.

While the test is meant to be fun, it should also have the desired effect of strengthening your own powers of perception no matter how well or badly you score.

Each answer contains a detailed analysis, not only to highlight the thought processes necessary to tackle each question, but to explore the reasons why you may not, in some cases, have arrived at the correct solution.

## Test of Perception

Time limit 30 minutes

1  How many circles and squares appear below?

2  The time is 19 minutes to the hour. Without looking at a clock, place the following in order reading anti-clockwise from the minute hand.

   II     XI     IX     III

3  Emphatically, famous frauds are the cause of many hours of frenzied yet fruitful scientific police research, combined with the experience of years.

   Count the number of times the letter F appears in the sentence above. You must count them just once and not recheck your answer.

4  Why are the words below in the order that they are?

   idea, knob, epic, hard, rare, wolf, sing, inch

5  Frank's mother had three children, The first was named June, the second was named May. What was the third child's name?

6  Imagine you are a bus driver. At the first stop, three females, four males and six children get on. At the second stop, four children and two females get on and one male gets off. At the third stop, one female gets on. How tall is the bus driver?

7  A famous Chinese conjuror claims that without bouncing a ping-pong ball off any surface or object and without tying anything to it, he can hit it with his hand propelling it a short distance, whereupon it will of its own accord come to a complete stop, and then come back straight to him. How does he perform this feat?

8  Alice sent the following cryptic message to the Cheshire Cat. Can you decode it?

nia gareh tego tyt pmu htu pt'nd luocn ems'g nikeh tllad nases rohs'g ni kehtl la

9  Apart from triangles and rectangles (4-sided geometric figures) do any other geometric figures appear below?

10  What is the connection between these pairs of words?

nomad ride

melon done

prom echo

chop arising

11  You cut a thick piece of wood into 12 equal pieces and stack them in two piles, each pile consisting of 6 pieces. You then find you have three piles of wood. Why?

12  Under any circumstances, is it ever legally possible for a man to marry his widow's daughter?

## Answers and answer analysis

1  No circles and no squares. Award yourself 4 points for a correct answer.

   Many people will look at the figure and assume that there are four black circles with their corners hidden by a white square. This is, in fact, an illusion created in the imagination of the beholder. All that actually appears are four three-quarter circles positioned in such a way as to give the illusion of a square. If you look closely, there is no square and there are no circles.

2  III      II      XI      IX        Award yourself 2 points for a
                                      correct answer.

   There is no trick here. People who get this wrong have usually read the question incorrectly, for example, 19 minutes *past* instead of 19 minutes *to* the hour, and reading *clockwise* instead of *anti-clockwise*. There is also a tendency to confuse the similar numerals II and III, and XI and IX.

3  9 times      Award yourself 2 points for a correct answer

   Surprisingly, on average, people only find six out of the nine on first reading. Many people tend to overlook the F in the word *of* since the brain sees it as V and not F.

4  The last letters of the words are ABCDEFGH
   Award yourself 2 points for a correct answer.

The requirement here is a perception and alertness of mind to look at the end of each word as well as the beginning, or the word as a whole. While the answer is there for all to see, to arrive quickly at this answer we must have the flexibility of mind to explore and analyse all possibilities.

5  Frank        Award yourself 3 points for a correct answer.

There are a number of distractions here which are deliberately designed to lead people into a false perception, even though we are told the answer in the first word of the question. First, we are presented with a seemingly logical sequence – June, May and then, presumably, April. We are also given the names of two girls and, therefore, automatically start to think that the third child is probably also a girl. By the time our mind has been cluttered up with these false perceptions, many will have forgotten that we are told in the opening statement that it is Frank's mother's children we are considering, and as two of her three children are named June and May, the name of her third and remaining child must be Frank himself.

6  Since you are the bus driver, then the bus driver is as tall as you are. Award yourself 3 points for a correct answer.

The film director Alfred Hitchcock used a technique in many of his movies which he called a McGuffin, that is, a story-line which turns out to be totally irrelevant to the remainder of the plot. Such a McGuffin was used in the film *Psycho*, where in the early part of the movie Marion Crane is shown stealing money from her employer and making off with it. She then checks into the Bates Motel, is murdered, and the stolen money is never referred to again. It becomes a forgotten and irrelevant part of the plot once it has served its purpose in getting Marion Crane to the Bates Motel.

This puzzle contains such a McGuffin. In the first sentence we are told that you, the reader, are the bus driver. In the final sentence you are asked the height of the bus driver, that is, yourself. The rest of the question is a complete irrelevance and merely there as a distraction in order to create a false perception of the question.

7   He hits the ball straight up in the air with his hand.
Award yourself 2 points for a correct answer.

Again there are McGuffins. The fact that he is a conjuror is irrelevant, as is the fact that he is Chinese. These facts are merely a distraction. It is necessary to pick the bones out of the question, which is to simply consider how it is possible to propel the ball so that it will travel but a short distance, come to a complete stop and then return to the sender.

8   Read the message backwards, altering word boundaries to uncover the message: *All the King's horses and all the King's men couldn't put Humpty together again.*   Award yourself 4 points for a correct answer

As with most of these puzzles the answer is there in front of you. However, as in the case of question 4, to arrive at this answer we must have sufficient flexibility of mind to explore quickly all possibilities. The tendency is to start analysing each set of letters individually. We tend to build artificial barriers in our minds between the groups of letters. However, the answer you are seeking must break down these barriers, since this then enables us to consider the message as a whole.

9

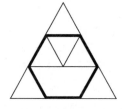

Award yourself 3 points for a correct answer.

The question leads us to assume, correctly, that at least one other geometric figure does appear. The problem is that this figure is not as easy to spot because it is disguised by having other figures within it, whereas the triangles and rectangle are not hidden in this way and stand out clearly for all to see.

10   The connection is capital cities of the world:

NO*MAD RID*E  –  Madrid

ME*LON DON*E  –  London

P*ROM E*CHO  –  Rome

CHO*PARIS*ING  –  Paris

Award yourself 3 points for a correct answer.

Once again, the answer is there for us to perceive. We are told in the question that we are looking for a *connection between* the *pairs* of words, and the answer is just such a connection. The problem is that many people tend to consider the words as a whole and not look for connecting parts of words. Again, it is necessary to break down these artificial barriers that the mind creates in order to find a solution.

11   The third pile is the sawdust from cutting up the wood.
Award yourself 4 points for a correct answer.

In this instance, it is necessary to employ a degree of lateral thinking in order to perceive more than just what the question tells us. The facts appear quite simple, twelve equal pieces (the fact that they are equal is another McGuffin) and two resultant piles of 6 pieces each. So, our first instinct is that the third pile of wood must have come from some outside source. It is only when we perceive in our mind the act of cutting up so many pieces from one thick piece that we realise that the third pile of wood must, in fact, be a pile of sawdust.

12  No, if he had a widow he would be dead, so could not marry
    anyone.        Award yourself 3 points for a correct answer.

   Again, there is a McGuffin. It is irrelevant to ask if it is legally
possible, but this irrelevance has the desired effect with many people
of providing a false perception of the problem and shifting the focus
of perspective away from the trap. The only thing which is relevant in
this case is that if the man has a widow, then he must be dead.

## Rating

| | |
|---|---|
| 30–35 | exceptionally perceptive |
| 25–29 | very perceptive |
| 20–28 | above average perception |
| 13–19 | average perception |
| 12 or less | below average perception |

# Part two

## Introduction

Part Two consists of 17 tests designed to assess different aspects of your personality.

In each test you are presented with 25 questions or statements about the aspect of your personality being assessed and you must respond with a simple *yes*, *no* or *don't know* answer.

There are no right or wrong answers and there is no time limit for completing the tests.

At all times respond to the question or statement as truthfully and realistically as possible in order to obtain an accurate assessment.

In the majority of cases you will be in a position to respond to each statement or question with a *yes* or *no* answer. However, on occasions you will be unsure of your response, in which case you should answer *don't know*.

# Kindness

Tick the appropriate column.

| | Yes | Don't know | No |
|---|---|---|---|
| 1 Would you support your friends if they were telling lies? | ❏ | ❏ | ❏ |
| 2 Do you not object to noisy children in your road? | ❏ | ❏ | ❏ |
| 3 Do you think that crimes should be punished less severely? | ❏ | ❏ | ❏ |
| 4 Are you kind to animals? | ❏ | ❏ | ❏ |
| 5 If your neighbour were sick would you do their shopping? | ❏ | ❏ | ❏ |
| 6 Are you sorry for victims of crime? | ❏ | ❏ | ❏ |
| 7 After a road accident, would you offer to drive people home? | ❏ | ❏ | ❏ |
| 8 If you found a child crying, would you try to find out the reason? | ❏ | ❏ | ❏ |

|   |   | Yes | Don't know | No |
|---|---|---|---|---|
| 9 | Are you sorry for people less fortunate than you? | ❏ | ❏ | ❏ |
| 10 | Would you help an old man crossing the road? | ❏ | ❏ | ❏ |
| 11 | Would you do the gardening for a disabled man or woman? | ❏ | ❏ | ❏ |
| 12 | Do you prefer the underdog? | ❏ | ❏ | ❏ |
| 13 | Do you give money to charity? | ❏ | ❏ | ❏ |
| 14 | Would you consider being a voluntary hospital visitor? | ❏ | ❏ | ❏ |
| 15 | Would you volunteer for 'Meals on Wheels'? | ❏ | ❏ | ❏ |
| 16 | If a neighbour's car were out of action, would you drive him or her to work? | ❏ | ❏ | ❏ |
| 17 | Would you carry a person's shopping to the car park? | ❏ | ❏ | ❏ |
| 18 | Do you give up your seat in a bus? | ❏ | ❏ | ❏ |
| 19 | Would you help somebody who has lost his way? | ❏ | ❏ | ❏ |
| 20 | Do you open doors for other people? | ❏ | ❏ | ❏ |

|  | Yes | Don't know | No |
|---|---|---|---|
| 21  Would you help a neighbour to mend his fence? | ❏ | ❏ | ❏ |
| 22  Are you always kind to sick people? | ❏ | ❏ | ❏ |
| 23  If a friend were short of money, would you give him some? | ❏ | ❏ | ❏ |
| 24  Have you ever lent money and not charged interest? | ❏ | ❏ | ❏ |
| 25  Would you give up your seat if somebody needed it more than you? | ❏ | ❏ | ❏ |

## Assessment

Award yourself 2 points for each *yes* answer, 1 point for each *don't know* answer and 0 points for each *no* answer.

### Less than 17 points

Although you do not lack the honesty to have answered the above questions accurately, your score indicates that kindness towards others is not one of your strong points.

This does not mean you are necessarily a cruel person, but it does mean that you should make an effort to show more concern for other people's feelings. We all have a kind side to our nature. However, it is sometimes necessary for some to work a little harder at developing it. This will not be perceived as being soft. Indeed, showing compassion for others and doing people the occasional good turn shows strength of character and can win you many new friends.

## 18–35 points

Although you occasionally may put your own desires and aspirations above all others, you are in the main a very reasonable and fair-minded person who genuinely tries to help other people in their time of need, and who has genuine compassion and sympathy for others at times of difficulty,

## 36–50 points

You appear to be an extremely kind person who genuinely shows a great deal of compassion for other people and always goes to great lengths to help anyone out who might be in distress, or needs a shoulder to cry on.

This will mean you have many friends who hold you in high esteem.

You should, however, try to make sure that no one tries to take advantage of your good nature. Although for you it is very difficult to say *no*, this may, on occasions, be necessary.

# Humour

Tick the appropriate column.

| | Yes | Don't know | No |
|---|---|---|---|
| 1 Do you tell risque jokes? | ❏ | ❏ | ❏ |
| 2 Do you play practical jokes? | ❏ | ❏ | ❏ |
| 3 Would you laugh if somebody trod on a banana skin? | ❏ | ❏ | ❏ |
| 4 Do you read joke books? | ❏ | ❏ | ❏ |
| 5 Do you often laugh aloud? | ❏ | ❏ | ❏ |
| 6 Do you laugh if somebody makes fun of you? | ❏ | ❏ | ❏ |
| 7 Would you smile if you saw a nude statue in an art gallery? | ❏ | ❏ | ❏ |
| 8 Do you like comedy films? | ❏ | ❏ | ❏ |
| 9 Would you sometimes laugh at yourself? | ❏ | ❏ | ❏ |

|                                                          | Yes | Don't know | No |
|----------------------------------------------------------|-----|------------|-----|
| 10  Would you order a strip-a-gram for a party?          | ❑   | ❑          | ❑   |
| 11  Do you smile at old Laurel and Hardy films?          | ❑   | ❑          | ❑   |
| 12  Do you laugh at practical jokes?                     | ❑   | ❑          | ❑   |
| 13  Are you rarely embarrassed?                          | ❑   | ❑          | ❑   |
| 14  Have you ever been intoxicated?                      | ❑   | ❑          | ❑   |
| 15  Do you prefer a comedy film to a mystery?            | ❑   | ❑          | ❑   |
| 16  Do you easily understand jokes?                      | ❑   | ❑          | ❑   |
| 17  Do you sometimes ridicule people?                    | ❑   | ❑          | ❑   |
| 18  Do you joke at work?                                 | ❑   | ❑          | ❑   |
| 19  Do you laugh at adversity?                           | ❑   | ❑          | ❑   |
| 20  Would you take a puncture in your stride?            | ❑   | ❑          | ❑   |
| 21  Would you like to be a comedian?                     | ❑   | ❑          | ❑   |
| 22  Do you laugh if you are caught out in the rain?      | ❑   | ❑          | ❑   |
| 23  Do you laugh at least once a day?                    | ❑   | ❑          | ❑   |

|  | Yes | Don't know | No |
|---|---|---|---|
| 24  Would you laugh at a joke, even if you had heard it before? | ❑ | ❑ | ❑ |
| 25  Do you laugh at circus clowns? | ❑ | ❑ | ❑ |

## Assessment

Award yourself 2 points for each *yes* answer, 1 point for each *don't know* answer and 0 points for each *no* answer.

### Less than 17 points

You appear to be of a rather serious nature and someone who does not particularly believe in seeing the funny side of things.

It is likely that you are quite introverted and hate the type of gatherings where everyone appears to be standing around shrieking with laughter for no apparent reason. When, however, something does amuse you, you are capable of breaking into laughter to the delight and bemusement of those around you, who rarely see this side of your nature.

You should remember that all of us are different, and many of us are amused by different things, and have different humour thresholds. Also, that sometimes it is necessary to try and see the funny side of many serious situations since this can help us get through them.

### 18–35 points

You are likely to have a very balanced sense of humour and are able to see the funny side of many situations, while at the same time being able to sympathise with people's misfortunes.

Although you have a straightforward approach to what makes you laugh, it does appear that you are quite selective in the type of things that do amuse you. Some people are offended by crude and vulgar jokes, while others find them funny, others like the banana peel type of humour while others would not dream of laughing at the misfortunes of others, and some respond to more sophisticated humour which causes no offence to others, such as subtle puns. An analysis of your individual responses to the questions in this test should give a clear indication of the type of humour that amuses you the most.

## 36–50 points

You have a very keen sense of fun which means that for the most part you progress through life with a good disposition.

This does not necessarily mean that you are easily amused by everything that happens around you, but it does mean that the things which you do find amusing, or can see the funny side of, are very wide ranging.

It may mean, however, that tact may not be one of your strong points, and that your amusement at, for example, the misfortunes of others may not always be appreciated, and in certain cases could cause offence.

That having been said, a good and wide-ranging sense of humour means that you have a wonderful outlook on life, and is likely to win you many friends, just so long as you take care not to offend anyone, and that you know when enough is enough.

# Jealousy/envy

Tick the appropriate column.

| | Yes | Don't know | No |
|---|:---:|:---:|:---:|
| 1 If a work-mate lived in a bigger house than you, would you be envious? | ❏ | ❏ | ❏ |
| 2 If you were under 5 ft 6 in in height, would you be envious of tall people? | ❏ | ❏ | ❏ |
| 3 Would you be jealous if you saw your partner talking to a person of the opposite sex? | ❏ | ❏ | ❏ |
| 4 Are you envious of a person with a better make of car? | ❏ | ❏ | ❏ |
| 5 Would you be envious of a person who is better looking than yourself? | ❏ | ❏ | ❏ |
| 6 At school were you envious of children who were cleverer than yourself? | ❏ | ❏ | ❏ |

|  |  | Yes | Don't know | No |
|---|---|---|---|---|
| 7 | Would you be envious if a friend won the Lottery? | ❏ | ❏ | ❏ |
| 8 | Do you consider that most people are luckier than you? | ❏ | ❏ | ❏ |
| 9 | Are you envious of people who attend more parties than yourself? | ❏ | ❏ | ❏ |
| 10 | Are you envious of rich people? | ❏ | ❏ | ❏ |
| 11 | Are you envious of famous people? | ❏ | ❏ | ❏ |
| 12 | Would you be envious if your neighbour had a better garden than yourself? | ❏ | ❏ | ❏ |
| 13 | Are you envious of people good at music? | ❏ | ❏ | ❏ |
| 14 | Are you envious of large families? | ❏ | ❏ | ❏ |
| 15 | Are you envious of Royalty? | ❏ | ❏ | ❏ |
| 16 | Are you envious of friends who are better at sports than you? | ❏ | ❏ | ❏ |
| 17 | Are you envious of people who went to university? | ❏ | ❏ | ❏ |
| 18 | Are you envious of people living a quiet life in the country? | ❏ | ❏ | ❏ |

|  | Yes | Don't know | No |
|---|---|---|---|
| 19　Are you envious of world-wide travellers? | ❏ | ❏ | ❏ |
| 20　Are you envious of anybody living in your road? | ❏ | ❏ | ❏ |
| 21　Are you envious if a friend has a much better job than yourself? | ❏ | ❏ | ❏ |
| 22　Are you envious of people who are tougher than yourself? | ❏ | ❏ | ❏ |
| 23　Are you envious of film stars? | ❏ | ❏ | ❏ |
| 24　Are you envious of religious people? | ❏ | ❏ | ❏ |
| 25　Are you envious of friends who can swim? | ❏ | ❏ | ❏ |

## Analysis

In psychology, jealousy is generally defined as an emotional state or anxiety due to a lack of sense of security in the affections of someone that you love. This jealousy is usually directed towards a third party, or rival, who appears to be gaining the affections of the object of love.

On the other hand, with envy there need be no loved ones, merely a desire for something possessed by another. This could take the form of material possessions, success, status or happiness.

## Assessment

Award yourself 2 points for each *yes* answer, 1 point for each *don't know* answer and 0 points for each *no* answer.

### Less than 17 points

You are not envious of other people and generally take little notice of their achievements, and are certainly not upset by the success of others.

You tend not to be impressed very easily, and when you are impressed you give credit where credit is due, but this has to be for something exceptional, rather than run-of-the mill everyday successes.

In general, you like to get on with your own life and let people get on with theirs. If they achieve success, then good luck to them.

### 18–35 points

You are not a jealous or envious person.

You are able to give credit when it is due, however, you do not particularly like boastful people, because you perceive this as a way of protecting feelings of inadequacy.

In general, you are likely to be satisfied with your own life, and do not envy other people's successes.

### 36–50 points

You can be envious of other people's successes and possessions.

For some people, jealousy and envy are part of their character, in other words, that is the way they are, and it is very difficult to change.

For other people, the feelings of envy are a result of not achieving what they expected out of life and of seeing others apparently achieving what they have failed to aspire to.

At such times it may be helpful to take stock of your own life and consider all the positive aspects, in other words, count your blessings. You will probably find that there are many. Also remember that success does not always bring happiness, and that contentment is indeed a virtue.

On the other hand, there is no harm in working harder and taking on important and difficult tasks, since the more you preoccupy yourself with them, the less time you will have to consider other people's achievements, and the less you will let other people's achievements upset you.

Remember that hard work does frequently bring with it the rewards of success. A top golfer was once accused of being lucky. 'Yes', he replied, 'and the harder I practise, the luckier I get.'

# Unafraid

Tick the appropriate column.

| | Yes | Don't know | No |
|---|---|---|---|
| 1 If you witnessed a mugging, would you chase the assailant? | ❏ | ❏ | ❏ |
| 2 Would you ride the 'Big Dipper' at the fairground? | ❏ | ❏ | ❏ |
| 3 Would you have liked to be an explorer? | ❏ | ❏ | ❏ |
| 4 Would you sleep in a haunted house? | ❏ | ❏ | ❏ |
| 5 Would you go out on your own at night? | ❏ | ❏ | ❏ |
| 6 Would you cuddle a white rat? | ❏ | ❏ | ❏ |
| 7 Would you argue with another driver in a road-rage situation? | ❏ | ❏ | ❏ |
| 8 Would you handle a snake? | ❏ | ❏ | ❏ |

|   |   | Yes | Don't know | No |
|---|---|---|---|---|
| 9 | Would you walk in a foreign jungle? | ❏ | ❏ | ❏ |
| 10 | Would you ride an elephant? | ❏ | ❏ | ❏ |
| 11 | Would you ride a horse? | ❏ | ❏ | ❏ |
| 12 | Would you place your hand into a box of maggots? | ❏ | ❏ | ❏ |
| 13 | Would you have the courage to work as a bomb disposal expert? | ❏ | ❏ | ❏ |
| 14 | Would you watch a horror film on television in the dark? | ❏ | ❏ | ❏ |
| 15 | Would you separate two dogs who were fighting? | ❏ | ❏ | ❏ |
| 16 | Would you keep a fierce dog? | ❏ | ❏ | ❏ |
| 17 | Would you go on a safari? | ❏ | ❏ | ❏ |
| 18 | Have you ever swum out of your depth? | ❏ | ❏ | ❏ |
| 19 | Have you ever climbed a high tree? | ❏ | ❏ | ❏ |
| 20 | Would you climb onto the roof of your house? | ❏ | ❏ | ❏ |
| 21 | Would you audition for a play? | ❏ | ❏ | ❏ |

|   |   | Don't |   |
|---|---|---|---|
|   | Yes | know | No |
| 22 Would you make a speech to a large audience? | ❑ | ❑ | ❑ |
| 23 Would you have the courage to be a deep-sea diver? | ❑ | ❑ | ❑ |
| 24 Would you drive a car at 150 mph? | ❑ | ❑ | ❑ |
| 25 Would you enter a quiz show? | ❑ | ❑ | ❑ |

## Analysis

Fear is an emotional state in the presence of a dangerous situation. It is usually characterised by extreme internal agitation together with a desire to flee the situation, or to attack, and by a variety of other reactions.

There is a subtle difference between fear and anxiety, in that fear involves specific objects or events, whereas anxiety is regarded as a more general state. Also, fear is a reaction to a present danger, whereas anxiety is a reaction to an anticipated or, even, an imagined one.

## Assessment

Award yourself 2 points for each *yes* answer, 1 point for each *don't know* answer and 0 points for each *no* answer.

### Less than 17 points

You are not very adventurous. In fact, you could, at times, be fairly described as being quite timid and reluctant to take any sort of chance in risky situations.

In some cases, however, it is necessary not just to have the courage of our own convictions but to stand up for ourselves and, now and again, steel ourselves to take a calculated risk.

Admittedly, this may prove difficult for you. However, doing something occasionally just for the hell of it can be a life-enriching experience and need not involve too much risk, and certainly need not mean risking life and limb.

## 18–35 points

You tend to be generally wary, but basically unafraid.

Although you do not take too many chances, if the situation did call for an act of bravery, you are likely to be to the fore.

In general, however, you prefer a quiet life without too much trouble. While not averse to taking the occasional risk, you prefer to do this in a measured, calculated way, having weighed up all the options first.

## 36–50 points

You have very strong nerves, which at times you need to keep in check since you may be inclined to throw caution to the wind.

You are likely to prove very good in an emergency and a good companion − a good person to have on someone's side.

It is very unlikely that anyone could ever accuse you of having led a dull life and your courage and the lifestyle you lead is likely to be admired by many. This is absolutely fine as long as you bear in mind the old adage of 'look before you leap'.

# Absent-minded

Tick the appropriate column.

|   |     | Yes | Don't know | No |
|---|-----|-----|------------|-----|
| 1 | Have you ever forgotten where you have parked your car? | ❏ | ❏ | ❏ |
| 2 | Do you forget to pay bills? | ❏ | ❏ | ❏ |
| 3 | Do you forget to pay debts? | ❏ | ❏ | ❏ |
| 4 | Do you often dream but have no recollection upon waking? | ❏ | ❏ | ❏ |
| 5 | Do you forget your next door neighbour's name? | ❏ | ❏ | ❏ |
| 6 | Have you frequently mislaid your keys? | ❏ | ❏ | ❏ |
| 7 | Do you sometimes mislay your possessions on a journey? | ❏ | ❏ | ❏ |
| 8 | Have you ever driven to the shops and walked back, forgetfully? | ❏ | ❏ | ❏ |

|     |                                                          | Yes | Don't know | No |
| --- | -------------------------------------------------------- | --- | ---------- | -- |
| 9   | Do you ever wear odd socks?                              | ❏   | ❏          | ❏  |
| 10  | Do you daydream?                                         | ❏   | ❏          | ❏  |
| 11  | Have you ever forgotten your telephone number?           | ❏   | ❏          | ❏  |
| 12  | Have you ever left an umbrella somewhere?                | ❏   | ❏          | ❏  |
| 13  | Have you often got lost while on holiday?                | ❏   | ❏          | ❏  |
| 14  | Have you ever forgotten your car number?                 | ❏   | ❏          | ❏  |
| 15  | Have you ever gone past your stop on a train?            | ❏   | ❏          | ❏  |
| 16  | Have you ever forgotten an address?                      | ❏   | ❏          | ❏  |
| 17  | Have you ever forgotten your mobile number?              | ❏   | ❏          | ❏  |
| 18  | Have you ever lost your credit card?                     | ❏   | ❏          | ❏  |
| 19  | Have you ever forgotten what day it is?                  | ❏   | ❏          | ❏  |
| 20  | Have you ever forgotten an appointment?                  | ❏   | ❏          | ❏  |

|    |                                                      | Yes | Don't know | No |
|----|------------------------------------------------------|-----|------------|-----|
| 21 | Have you ever misplaced your driving licence?        | ❑   | ❑          | ❑   |
| 22 | Do you ever get names mixed up?                      | ❑   | ❑          | ❑   |
| 23 | Have you ever lost your wallet?                      | ❑   | ❑          | ❑   |
| 24 | Are you not good at remembering birthdays and anniversaries? | ❑   | ❑          | ❑   |
| 25 | Do you have to make a list when you go shopping?     | ❑   | ❑          | ❑   |

## Assessment

Award yourself 2 points for each *yes* answer, 1 point for each *don't know* answer and 0 points for each *no* answer.

### Less than 17 points

You are likely to have an extremely good memory with a very orderly mind and high powers of concentration.

### 18–35 points

In general, you cannot be described as being absent-minded and rarely forget such things as important meetings and activities.

While your concentration is above average you should perhaps discipline yourself to make lists of activities that you need to undertake and set yourself targets for completing them

## *36–50 points*

Your score indicates that you are, at times, somewhat absent-minded.

The reason for this could be that you have a very active mind and tend to think of many different things at once.

Perhaps you should discipline yourself to focus your energy on completing one task at a time and not let your mind wander onto other things. Also, you could, perhaps, try slowing down just a little.

It may help you to make lists continually, for example, of tasks that need to be completed or of items you require when visiting the supermarket, or items you need to pack when going away on holiday.

You should also keep a diary and refer to it frequently.

# Justice

Tick the appropriate column.

|   |   | Yes | Don't know | No |
|---|---|:---:|:---:|:---:|
| 1 | Do you think that the punishment should fit the crime? | ❑ | ❑ | ❑ |
| 2 | Do you think that sentences in the courts are fair? | ❑ | ❑ | ❑ |
| 3 | Do you think that prison is for rehabilitation? | ❑ | ❑ | ❑ |
| 4 | Do you believe that if a person in high office has defaulted, then he should be removed? | ❑ | ❑ | ❑ |
| 5 | Do you believe that prisoners should have their sentences reduced if they have behaved well? | ❑ | ❑ | ❑ |
| 6 | Do you support the underdog? | ❑ | ❑ | ❑ |
| 7 | Do you not believe in capital punishment? | ❑ | ❑ | ❑ |

| | Yes | Don't know | No |
|---|---|---|---|
| 8   Would you like to see prison ships anchored off shore? | ❑ | ❑ | ❑ |
| 9   Do you always abide by the rules? | ❑ | ❑ | ❑ |
| 10   Would you break the law to help a friend? | ❑ | ❑ | ❑ |
| 11   Do you think that judges are out of touch with modern-day events? | ❑ | ❑ | ❑ |
| 12   If you were a judge, would you be tolerant? | ❑ | ❑ | ❑ |
| 13   Would you not object if a juvenile delinquent home opened in your road? | ❑ | ❑ | ❑ |
| 14   Would you like to be a policeman? | ❑ | ❑ | ❑ |
| 15   Do you believe in the triumph of good over evil? | ❑ | ❑ | ❑ |
| 16   Do you believe that a life sentence means just that? | ❑ | ❑ | ❑ |
| 17   Would you own up to a wrong-doing? | ❑ | ❑ | ❑ |
| 18   Do you think that money stolen should be returned after sentence? | ❑ | ❑ | ❑ |

|  | Yes | Don't know | No |
|---|---|---|---|
| 19  Do you believe that one good turn deserves another? | ❑ | ❑ | ❑ |
| 20  Would you like to see the stocks returned to the market place? | ❑ | ❑ | ❑ |
| 21  Do you believe that criminals under 14 years should not be punished by prison? | ❑ | ❑ | ❑ |
| 22  Do you believe that a first offence should always be punished? | ❑ | ❑ | ❑ |
| 23  Would you not sentence a man down on his luck? | ❑ | ❑ | ❑ |
| 24  Do you like policemen? | ❑ | ❑ | ❑ |
| 25  Do you believe that the law is an ass? | ❑ | ❑ | ❑ |

## Assessment

Award yourself 2 points for each *yes* answer, 1 point for each *don't know* answer and 0 points for each *no* answer.

### Less than 17 points

You are a very fair-minded person but at times could find yourself disagreeing with the establishment, and while having a strong sense of justice, your inclinations are often towards the side of the underdog.

As such, you have a strong sense of fair play and a belief that society has a duty to seek out continually the root causes of crime and reform criminals where possible. You see at all times a need to get to the heart of society's problems, and this is as important to you as the need to see criminals get their just deserts.

This is not to suggest you have a soft attitude towards crime, but it does mean you believe everyone has a right to a fair trial and receive appropriate punishment if found guilty.

## 18–35 points

You firmly believe in right and wrong and have a very fair and balanced sense of justice.

While you are not necessarily a hard-liner as far as justice is concerned, and not someone who believes we should lock people in jail and throw away the key, you do believe that punishment should fit the crime and that justice for all is crucially important to our society.

Although at times you may have a rebellious streak yourself, you are generally firmly on the side of law and order.

## 36–50 points

You have a strong sense of justice and of what is right, and what is wrong, in our society.

This does also mean that you are in the main very intolerant of transgressors within our society. You are likely to be a firm believer in tough sentencing and possibly believe that we are often too soft when sentencing offenders, and that to a great extent this soft approach is one of the root causes of the current high level of crime and indiscipline within our society.

You are also not convinced that it is possible to reform the most serious offenders and believe that it is impossible to change the way some people are.

The question of justice is, to you, of great importance and is something which much occupies your thoughts.

# Friendship

Tick the appropriate column.

|  | Yes | Don't know | No |
|---|---|---|---|
| 1 Do you still keep in touch with old friends at school? | ❑ | ❑ | ❑ |
| 2 Would you lend money to an old friend who had fallen on hard times? | ❑ | ❑ | ❑ |
| 3 Have you more than 10 close friends? | ❑ | ❑ | ❑ |
| 4 Do you go on holiday with friends rather than alone with your family? | ❑ | ❑ | ❑ |
| 5 Have you close friends at work? | ❑ | ❑ | ❑ |
| 6 Do you make friends easily? | ❑ | ❑ | ❑ |
| 7 Do you belong to social clubs? | ❑ | ❑ | ❑ |
| 8 Would you tell a friend if their partner were having an affair? | ❑ | ❑ | ❑ |
| 9 Would you confide in a friend if you were in trouble? | ❑ | ❑ | ❑ |

|    |                                                              | Yes | Don't know | No |
|----|--------------------------------------------------------------|-----|------------|----|
| 10 | Would you lie to get a friend out of a court case?           | ❏   | ❏          | ❏  |
| 11 | Would you take advice from a friend?                         | ❏   | ❏          | ❏  |
| 12 | Have you a major friend?                                     | ❏   | ❏          | ❏  |
| 13 | Do you get jealous of people very easily?                    | ❏   | ❏          | ❏  |
| 14 | If two friends were arguing, would you try to appease them?  | ❏   | ❏          | ❏  |
| 15 | Would you be pleased if a friend won promotion?              | ❏   | ❏          | ❏  |
| 16 | Do you trust a friend?                                       | ❏   | ❏          | ❏  |
| 17 | Would you admire a friend's car?                             | ❏   | ❏          | ❏  |
| 18 | Have you more friends than enemies?                          | ❏   | ❏          | ❏  |
| 19 | If a friend were ill would you visit him or her in hospital frequently? | ❏ | ❏ | ❏  |
| 20 | Would you organise a 'Neighbourhood Watch' scheme?          | ❏   | ❏          | ❏  |
| 21 | Would you ever consider a friend as part of the family?     | ❏   | ❏          | ❏  |

|    |                                                              | Yes | Don't know | No |
|----|--------------------------------------------------------------|-----|------------|-----|
| 22 | Would you be pleased if a friend won the Lottery?            | ❑   | ❑          | ❑  |
| 23 | Would you trust a friend with your life?                     | ❑   | ❑          | ❑  |
| 24 | Do you always do friends favours?                           | ❑   | ❑          | ❑  |
| 25 | If a friend were ill, would you look after the friend's garden? | ❑   | ❑          | ❑  |

## Assessment

Award yourself 2 points for each *yes* answer, 1 point for each *don't know* answer and 0 points for each *no* answer.

### Less than 17 points

While you may be what some people describe as a loner, it is possible that the friends you do have are very close and long-term, and these people are quite likely to value your friendship greatly, as you value theirs.

It is quite possible you are a very introverted person and this is why you do not make friends easily.

If this is a problem for you, and it may not be necessarily, then the only way to make more friends is to become more outgoing and mix with people more, either by joining a club, taking up a sport or some other hobby, or by cultivating an interest and finding a way to meet other people who share the same interest.

It is also possible that you might not be as kind and considerate to other people as you should be. While this may not be intentional on your part, it could be the one reason why you do not make many close and long-term friends, and it may, therefore, be something you need to think about carefully and analyse why some of the friendships you did form in the past only survived for a very short period.

## 18–35 points

While you do not actively go out of your way to seek new friends, the friendships that you have formed over the years are likely to be important and highly valued with a mutual bond of trust and support when necessary.

You probably appreciate that friendship is very important in all our lives, and that in difficult times we can all benefit from the support of people we can trust.

## 36–50 points

The friendship of other people is extremely important to you and as such you are likely to have a wide circle of friends, and be able to cultivate many new friendships in the future.

It is probable that you are an outgoing and extrovert person who finds it easy to converse with people and make friends easily.

While this means that you are regarded as a very sociable, and probably very kind, person who is well liked, it could also mean that there are a great many people who you describe as friends, but very few of these who you can describe as close friends. You should ensure that you are able to distinguish between these mere acquaintances, and the really close friends in whom you can put your trust, and turn to, in times of need.

# Anxiety

Tick the appropriate column.

|   | | Yes | Don't know | No |
|---|---|---|---|---|
| 1 | Do you worry on long train journeys? | ❏ | ❏ | ❏ |
| 2 | If you play football, would you not be taking penalties? | ❏ | ❏ | ❏ |
| 3 | Are you a nervous driver? | ❏ | ❏ | ❏ |
| 4 | Are you nervous at job interviews? | ❏ | ❏ | ❏ |
| 5 | Do you worry about finance? | ❏ | ❏ | ❏ |
| 6 | Do you frequently visit your doctor? | ❏ | ❏ | ❏ |
| 7 | Would you not sing solo at a party? | ❏ | ❏ | ❏ |
| 8 | Do you worry about losing your hair? | ❏ | ❏ | ❏ |
| 9 | Are you self-conscious? | ❏ | ❏ | ❏ |

|  | Yes | Don't know | No |
|---|---|---|---|
| 10  Are you not prepared to take on responsibility at work? | ❏ | ❏ | ❏ |
| 11  Would you not take part in a play? | ❏ | ❏ | ❏ |
| 12  Do you worry about trifling things? | ❏ | ❏ | ❏ |
| 13  Do you worry about making a speech? | ❏ | ❏ | ❏ |
| 14  Do you not always remember your car number? | ❏ | ❏ | ❏ |
| 15  Do you sometimes forget appointments? | ❏ | ❏ | ❏ |
| 16  Do you not remember names? | ❏ | ❏ | ❏ |
| 17  Have you ever passed your station on a train? | ❏ | ❏ | ❏ |
| 18  Do you not remember birthdays? | ❏ | ❏ | ❏ |
| 19  Do you bite your fingernails? | ❏ | ❏ | ❏ |
| 20  Do you follow a regular diet? | ❏ | ❏ | ❏ |
| 21  Do you not sleep well? | ❏ | ❏ | ❏ |
| 22  Do you get upset if people mock you? | ❏ | ❏ | ❏ |

|  | Yes | Don't know | No |
|---|:---:|:---:|:---:|
| 23 Do you pay your bills immediately they arrive? | ❑ | ❑ | ❑ |
| 24 Do you worry over little things? | ❑ | ❑ | ❑ |
| 25 Do you sometimes forget your telephone number? | ❑ | ❑ | ❑ |

## Assessment

Award yourself 2 points for each *yes* answer, 1 point for each *don't know* answer and 0 points for each *no* answer.

### Less than 17 points

Anxiety is less of a problem for you than it is for the average person.

You are in the fortunate position of having an extremely laid-back attitude to life in general and are not inclined to worry about trivialities.

This attitude can have a calming influence not just on yourself, but on those around you.

While you are ready to spring into action when the need arises, you should take care not to be naive to the point of believing that problems will never occur. Often, if we do anticipate problems, then we can avoid them, so on occasions a degree of forward planning and a certain amount of caution is desirable.

### 18–35 points

Although, like all of us, you find yourself stressed out to a certain degree from time to time, you are generally a well-balanced person who tackles problems as they arise and does not spend all their time worrying about things which may never happen.

You do not tend to worry about unimportant trifles and build these things up out of all proportion, and you have sufficient resolve to face up to any eventualities that may be lurking around the corner.

## 36–50 points

You find it very difficult to relax completely and you are constantly on your toes ready for any unforeseen event that may occur.

It is important that you try to adopt a more relaxed attitude to life, difficult as this may seem, since anxiety does lead to stress, and stress is the cause of many serious health problems.

You should make a concerted effort to relax more and keep calm in all situations. This may be achieved by cultivating a new interest or pastime, and by taking one step back and reflecting on your life and its positive aspects.

In times of extreme anxiety, try to switch off completely and relax doing something you really enjoy. This should enable you to get things into proportion and help you to cultivate a more relaxed attitude to life in general.

# Artistic

Tick the appropriate column.

|  | Yes | Don't know | No |
|---|---|---|---|
| 1 Do you appreciate the Cubism school of painting? | ❑ | ❑ | ❑ |
| 2 Do you like Picasso's work? | ❑ | ❑ | ❑ |
| 3 Would you like to be an architect? | ❑ | ❑ | ❑ |
| 4 Are you good at flower arranging? | ❑ | ❑ | ❑ |
| 5 Can you lay an attractive table? | ❑ | ❑ | ❑ |
| 6 Are you interested in landscape gardening? | ❑ | ❑ | ❑ |
| 7 Can you draw a recognisable sketch of a friend? | ❑ | ❑ | ❑ |
| 8 Would you regularly visit art galleries? | ❑ | ❑ | ❑ |
| 9 Would you go to painting classes? | ❑ | ❑ | ❑ |

|  | | Yes | Don't know | No |
|---|---|---|---|---|
| 10 | Do you possess a board and easel? | ❏ | ❏ | ❏ |
| 11 | Do you dress in the latest fashion? | ❏ | ❏ | ❏ |
| 12 | Is your garden nicely landscaped? | ❏ | ❏ | ❏ |
| 13 | Would you go to sculpture classes? | ❏ | ❏ | ❏ |
| 14 | Have you heard of the Fibonacci Series? | ❏ | ❏ | ❏ |
| 15 | Would you like to have been a dress designer? | ❏ | ❏ | ❏ |
| 16 | Have you a flair for fashion? | ❏ | ❏ | ❏ |
| 17 | Would you like to have been born in Edwardian times? | ❏ | ❏ | ❏ |
| 18 | Is one of your hobbies painting? | ❏ | ❏ | ❏ |
| 19 | Do you do your own decorating? | ❏ | ❏ | ❏ |
| 20 | Do you visit art galleries on holiday? | ❏ | ❏ | ❏ |
| 21 | Do you spend too much on flowers for the garden? | ❏ | ❏ | ❏ |
| 22 | Could you design a set for a play? | ❏ | ❏ | ❏ |
| 23 | Do you belong to an amateur dramatic society? | ❏ | ❏ | ❏ |

|  | Yes | Don't know | No |
|---|---|---|---|
| 24 Would you ride on a float at a carnival? | ❑ | ❑ | ❑ |
| 25 Do you know the colour if blue mixes with yellow? | ❑ | ❑ | ❑ |

## Analysis

### *Art is life and life is art*

Because they are such diverse and wide-ranging subjects, it is difficult to measure both artistic flair and appreciation of the arts, and creativity.

The subject of both laterality and creativity have been explored in more depth in Part 1, as well as the fact that the human brain consists of two identical hemispheres, and that it is the right side of these hemispheres which controls spatial ability, artistic appreciation and creative thought.

Because it is so unpressured and uncluttered, it is in a young child that the mind is at its most creative, since the child instinctively uses both hemispheres of the brain, and learns an enormous amount of information and skills during these early years, without formal training. This rapid development can, however, slow down when the child reaches the education system, which generally concentrates on the left side of the brain. Thus, by the time the child has reached early adulthood the creative right hemisphere has been taken over by the more dominant left hemisphere, the hemisphere that controls language, order, sequence and logic, simply because it was not given enough opportunity to function.

Educationalists, therefore, have a duty to encourage creative and artistic talents in all young people. However, this is not always the case. In today's world of specialisation many of these early talents are stifled and energies are channelled into one specific career, with the result that many latent talents remain underdeveloped.

This test is designed to identify artistic skills and appreciation in a number of areas to give an overall assessment of your artistic flair. Similarly, the test of creativity that follows is designed to identify to what extent you are using your creative talents.

Since we all have a right side to our brains, we all have the potential to be creative and artistic. Until we try, we never really know what we can achieve.

## Assessment

Award yourself 2 points for each *yes* answer, 1 point for each *don't know* answer and 0 points for each *no* answer.

### Less than 17 points

Your score indicates that in general you have little interest in the artistic elements.

It is likely that you are quite a down-to-earth person who has little time for things which you consider extravagant, or for the finer details of our existence.

An appreciation of art can, however, provide many stimulating and uplifting experiences, and may enable you to discover that you have many hidden talents. There is a whole new world out there waiting to be explored. By cultivating new ideas and interests it is possible for each of us to exploit the potential of the often underused parts of the human brain.

### 18–35 points

Although you have an appreciation of art in general, it may be that the artistic side of your life has never blossomed.

Since you appear to have a good knowledge of the artistic world, you should try your hand at artistic pursuits because you may find some hidden talent.

You are able to appreciate the finer details of existence.

## 36–50 points

You have a good and wide understanding of our world and are capable of seeing beauty in the most unusual places.

If you have not already done so, you should endeavour to explore and exploit your artistic appreciation and flair.

# Creativity

Tick the appropriate column.

| | Yes | Don't know | No |
|---|---|---|---|
| 1 Are you good at drawing or painting? | ❑ | ❑ | ❑ |
| 2 Do you belong to a drama group? | ❑ | ❑ | ❑ |
| 3 Would you like to be an artist? | ❑ | ❑ | ❑ |
| 4 Have you a nicely designed garden? | ❑ | ❑ | ❑ |
| 5 Have you been to an art gallery in the last year? | ❑ | ❑ | ❑ |
| 6 Are you a good chess player? | ❑ | ❑ | ❑ |
| 7 Have you ever belonged to a pottery class? | ❑ | ❑ | ❑ |
| 8 Do you wear the latest style in dress? | ❑ | ❑ | ❑ |
| 9 Would you like to be an inventor? | ❑ | ❑ | ❑ |

|    |                                              | Yes | Don't know | No |
|----|----------------------------------------------|:---:|:----------:|:--:|
| 10 | Do you read glossy home magazines?           | ❏   | ❏          | ❏  |
| 11 | Do you own a library ticket?                 | ❏   | ❏          | ❏  |
| 12 | Have you ever written a short story?         | ❏   | ❏          | ❏  |
| 13 | Are you a lover of poetry?                   | ❏   | ❏          | ❏  |
| 14 | Do you visit stately homes?                  | ❏   | ❏          | ❏  |
| 15 | Do you like flower arranging?                | ❏   | ❏          | ❏  |
| 16 | Are you a keen gardener?                      | ❏   | ❏          | ❏  |
| 17 | Do you believe in ESP (extrasensory perception)? | ❏ | ❏        | ❏  |
| 18 | Would you like to work in the film industry? | ❏   | ❏          | ❏  |
| 19 | Would you like to be a cartoonist?           | ❏   | ❏          | ❏  |
| 20 | Are you a DIY expert?                        | ❏   | ❏          | ❏  |
| 21 | Have you ever had music lessons?             | ❏   | ❏          | ❏  |
| 22 | Did you enjoy acting in plays at school?     | ❏   | ❏          | ❏  |
| 23 | Have you ever composed poetry?               | ❏   | ❏          | ❏  |

|  | Yes | Don't know | No |
|---|---|---|---|
| 24  Are you good at crossword puzzles? | ❏ | ❏ | ❏ |
| 25  Do you play a musical instrument? | ❏ | ❏ | ❏ |

## Assessment

Award yourself 2 points for each *yes* answer, 1 point for each *don't know* answer and 0 points for each *no* answer.

### Less than 17 points

Although we all have the potential to be creative, it appears that, like many other people, you have not explored your creative talents.

It is quite likely that your skill outlets have been channelled into one particular area in order to develop a career, and that, therefore, you are a specialist who has little time to explore other things.

By exploring new avenues, however, it should be possible to broaden your horizons considerably and, possibly, discover that you possess many creative talents of which you were unaware.

Go on — surprise yourself!

### 18–35 points

You exhibit creative leanings, although it is possible that you neither have the time, nor the confidence, to explore your creative urges.

As such, your creativity remains somewhat on hold, and will do so until you take the plunge and try your hand at some creative pursuit such as painting, or writing that novel you always felt was inside you.

Life is not a rehearsal. If you do not try out different things now you may never know what you might achieve ... .

## 36–50 points

The creative side of your brain seems well to the fore.

This is wonderful, providing you occasionally come back down to earth and do not forget the importance of developing your analytical and intellectual skills as well as your creative talents.

It is likely you have tried out many creative pursuits during your lifetime and will continue to do so in the coming years since you are never afraid of trying out something new.

It is also possible that you will, or have, achieved success and fulfilment within a creative environment, for example, as a writer, designer or in the theatre.

If you have not tried creative pursuits such as painting, garden design or music in the past, then you should do so now whenever you get the urge, since you appear to have the necessary skills which may have been lying dormant, and you also may have major undeveloped talents waiting to surface.

# Thrifty

Tick the appropriate column.

| | Yes | Don't know | No |
|---|---|---|---|
| 1  Are you good at paying bills promptly? | ❏ | ❏ | ❏ |
| 2  Do you avoid paying car park fees by walking? | ❏ | ❏ | ❏ |
| 3  Do you avoid gambling? | ❏ | ❏ | ❏ |
| 4  Do you regularly save an amount of money? | ❏ | ❏ | ❏ |
| 5  Do you owe a small amount on your credit card? | ❏ | ❏ | ❏ |
| 6  Do you haggle at the market? | ❏ | ❏ | ❏ |
| 7  Do you remember to switch off lights? | ❏ | ❏ | ❏ |
| 8  Do you buy cheap offers at food shops? | ❏ | ❏ | ❏ |

|  |  | Yes | Don't know | No |
|---|---|---|---|---|
| 9 | Do you know how much approximately your bank balance is? | ❏ | ❏ | ❏ |
| 10 | If you won the Lottery, would you give more than half away? | ❏ | ❏ | ❏ |
| 11 | Do you look for bargains? | ❏ | ❏ | ❏ |
| 12 | Do you buy on impulse? | ❏ | ❏ | ❏ |
| 13 | Do you squeeze out the last drop of toothpaste? | ❏ | ❏ | ❏ |
| 14 | Do you drive at the most economical speed to suit petrol consumption? | ❏ | ❏ | ❏ |
| 15 | Do you have a yearly car overhaul? | ❏ | ❏ | ❏ |
| 16 | Do you have your shoes repaired regularly? | ❏ | ❏ | ❏ |
| 17 | Is your wardrobe nearly empty? | ❏ | ❏ | ❏ |
| 18 | Are all of your electrical appliances insured against failure? | ❏ | ❏ | ❏ |
| 19 | Do you save half-empty paint cans? | ❏ | ❏ | ❏ |
| 20 | Are you economical with water? | ❏ | ❏ | ❏ |
| 21 | Do you frequently use second-class stamps? | ❏ | ❏ | ❏ |

| | Yes | Don't know | No |
|---|---|---|---|
| 22  Do you save envelopes for re-use? | ❏ | ❏ | ❏ |
| 23  Do you use tea bags more than once? | ❏ | ❏ | ❏ |
| 24  Do you make lengthy phone calls? | ❏ | ❏ | ❏ |
| 25  Do you have an allotment? | ❏ | ❏ | ❏ |

## Assessment

Award yourself 2 points for each *yes* answer, 1 point for each *don't know* answer and 0 points for each *no* answer.

### Less than 17 points

You certainly cannot be described as being a thrifty person, in fact your score indicates that you are likely to be an extremely generous spender, and this will endear you to many people.

It may mean, however, that you are less than careful, even at times careless, in money matters and live for the day, rather than planning for the future. This can often lead to problems.

You should try to discipline yourself more as far as finance is concerned, and possibly try to put a little aside each week for a rainy day.

### 18–35 points

While you do not squander money, you are not afraid to splash out on the occasional luxury item.

While you appear to be well in control of your finances, you should also be aware of the need always to plan for the future, as well as enjoying the present.

## 36–50 points

You appear to be quite a thrifty person. This is fine, and should mean that you are always likely to be financially secure, and have a nest egg put aside for a rainy day, just as long as money does not become something of an obsession. If this did happen, you would be likely to start worrying about your financial status no matter how financially secure you were and you would be reluctant to spend anything.

You should, on occasion, sample the pleasures of not having to watch every penny that you spend. While money cannot buy complete happiness, it can buy many luxuries and treats from which one can derive a great deal of pleasure.

# Impulsive

Tick the appropriate column.

|  | Yes | Don't know | No |
|---|---|---|---|
| 1  Have you ever wagered a large sum of money on a horse race? | ❏ | ❏ | ❏ |
| 2  Have you ever purchased something that you do not really need? | ❏ | ❏ | ❏ |
| 3  Do you like the look of a person on a first meeting? | ❏ | ❏ | ❏ |
| 4  Do you judge people on a first assessment of their character? | ❏ | ❏ | ❏ |
| 5  Do you spend more than you earn? | ❏ | ❏ | ❏ |
| 6  Do you ever jump the traffic lights? | ❏ | ❏ | ❏ |
| 7  Would you gamble on the toss of a coin? | ❏ | ❏ | ❏ |
| 8  Do you sometimes buy an article that you cannot really afford? | ❏ | ❏ | ❏ |

|   |   | Yes | Don't know | No |
|---|---|---|---|---|
| 9 | Do you sometimes make decisions without really thinking them out? | ❑ | ❑ | ❑ |
| 10 | Would you work at a dangerous job? | ❑ | ❑ | ❑ |
| 11 | Do you sometimes do things on the spur of the moment? | ❑ | ❑ | ❑ |
| 12 | Would you tell a lie at work where you could be found out? | ❑ | ❑ | ❑ |
| 13 | Do you sometimes change your mind on the spur of the moment? | ❑ | ❑ | ❑ |
| 14 | Would you take unnecessary risks? | ❑ | ❑ | ❑ |
| 15 | Would you separate two men who were fighting? | ❑ | ❑ | ❑ |
| 16 | Do you sometimes say something which afterwards you are sorry for? | ❑ | ❑ | ❑ |
| 17 | Do you jump to conclusions? | ❑ | ❑ | ❑ |
| 18 | Do you stop to think before taking action? | ❑ | ❑ | ❑ |
| 19 | Do you often change your mind? | ❑ | ❑ | ❑ |
| 20 | Do you make a decision and sometimes regret it afterwards? | ❑ | ❑ | ❑ |

|  |  | Don't |  |
|  | Yes | know | No |
| 21  Would you accept a dare? | ❏ | ❏ | ❏ |
| 22  Would you jump over a stream? | ❏ | ❏ | ❏ |
| 23  Do you take action without really thinking first? | ❏ | ❏ | ❏ |
| 24  Would you adopt a stray dog? | ❏ | ❏ | ❏ |
| 25  Do you decide something on the spur of the moment or stop and think it through? | ❏ | ❏ | ❏ |

## Assessment

Award yourself 2 points for each *yes* answer, 1 point for each *don't know* answer and 0 points for each *no* answer.

### Less than 17 points

Your motto appears to be *safety first always* and you certainly cannot be described as being in any way impulsive.

You weigh up and consider every aspect of a situation before reaching a decision and sometimes sleep on things for almost an eternity.

While this is a commendable trait, and leads to a safe life, it can often also lead to indecision.

There are times in all our lives when we need to take a chance, and there are other times when we must make snap decisions. When the occasion demands it, we must all have the courage to act on impulse.

## 18–35 points

You are no more impulsive than the average person.

You are careful and steady, yet prone to making occasional decisions that have not been thought through to completion.

At all times, try to retain the right balance between two old adages – *look before you leap* and *he who hesitates is lost*.

## 36–50 points

You seem to act more on impulse than thinking things through to the end.

Good judgement is, however, generally much more desirable and is likely to achieve much better results than acting on impulse.

Instead of being tempted to jump in too soon, even to the extent of going off like a loose cannon, you should try a more restrained approach and think things through to a safe conclusion.

Often, what seems like a good idea when it suddenly occurs to you, can prove impracticable when thought through carefully and slept upon.

# Extroverted

Tick the appropriate column.

|  | Yes | Don't know | No |
|---|---|---|---|
| 1  Do you play dangerous sports? | ❏ | ❏ | ❏ |
| 2  Would you like to be a film director? | ❏ | ❏ | ❏ |
| 3  Would you like to pilot a plane? | ❏ | ❏ | ❏ |
| 4  Would you like to appear on live television? | ❏ | ❏ | ❏ |
| 5  Would you like to be a comedian? | ❏ | ❏ | ❏ |
| 6  Do you go to night clubs? | ❏ | ❏ | ❏ |
| 7  Would you sing solo at a large gathering of family and friends? | ❏ | ❏ | ❏ |
| 8  Would you like to be a racing driver? | ❏ | ❏ | ❏ |
| 9  Would you tell the manager at work if he were wrong? | ❏ | ❏ | ❏ |

|    |                                                                       | Yes | Don't know | No |
|----|-----------------------------------------------------------------------|-----|------------|-----|
| 10 | Did you or would you make a good speech at your wedding?              | ❏   | ❏          | ❏   |
| 11 | Could you organise a party?                                           | ❏   | ❏          | ❏   |
| 12 | Do you hold a responsible position at work?                          | ❏   | ❏          | ❏   |
| 13 | Would you like to take a parachute jump?                             | ❏   | ❏          | ❏   |
| 14 | Are you a good public speaker?                                       | ❏   | ❏          | ❏   |
| 15 | Would you like to work in a high-pressure finance job in the City?   | ❏   | ❏          | ❏   |
| 16 | Would you stand for a constituency in politics?                      | ❏   | ❏          | ❏   |
| 17 | Would you like to be Mayor of your town?                             | ❏   | ❏          | ❏   |
| 18 | Did you stand up to a bully at school?                               | ❏   | ❏          | ❏   |
| 19 | Would you swim naked on holiday?                                     | ❏   | ❏          | ❏   |
| 20 | Would you volunteer for a rescue party?                              | ❏   | ❏          | ❏   |
| 21 | Would you like to lead a mountaineering team?                        | ❏   | ❏          | ❏   |

| | Yes | Don't know | No |
|---|---|---|---|
| 22 Would you like to be a star performer at a circus? | ❑ | ❑ | ❑ |
| 23 Would you like to be an actor? | ❑ | ❑ | ❑ |
| 24 Would you take a deciding penalty kick in a soccer match? | ❑ | ❑ | ❑ |
| 25 Do you enjoy being the centre of attention? | ❑ | ❑ | ❑ |

## Assessment

Award yourself 2 points for each *yes* answer, 1 point for each *don't know* answer and 0 points for each *no* answer.

### Less than 17 points

Your score indicates that you are quite introverted and what people might sometimes refer to as a shrinking violet.

This does not, of course, make you any worse a person than someone who is excessively outgoing.

In many ways you are a shy person and like to keep your views to yourself. On some occasions when you do wish to express an opinion or join in a conversation, you may be afraid of doing so, because you worry about what people may think, especially if there are several people present. This is indicative of a lack of confidence in yourself even to the extent of a feeling of inferiority.

This does not mean that you cannot be successful in life, since many people who are extremely introverted and modest have the ability to be high achievers in their own field.

You should try to gain that extra bit of self-confidence to harness your potential even more and try not to be backward at coming forward.

Try letting your hair down once in a while.

## 18–35 points

You are neither extrovert nor introvert and appear to be well balanced and content to take the middle field.

While you may not go out of your way to seek leadership in events, you are supportive and unafraid of new experiences.

Although you may sometimes wish that you could be as outgoing as those who are more extrovert than yourself, it may well be that by having the ability to show a little reserve at the right time you are probably regarded by other people as someone whom they prefer having in their company.

## 36–50 points

Your motto seems to be *life is for living*.

You are very much an extrovert and likely to be a leader, or aspire to be a leader, in most fields.

You will certainly not be lacking in confidence, and always aim to make the most of life. You are the life and soul of every party and enjoy meeting people and forming new friendships.

Although many people will admire your zest and energy, you should at the same time ensure that you do not appear excessively pushy, even overbearing. Your energy and extroversion will bring you even greater success and many more friends if it is tempered with some degree of modesty and sensitivity towards others.

# Success

Tick the appropriate column.

| | Yes | Don't know | No |
|---|---|---|---|
| 1 Are you able to focus on one thing at a time? | ❑ | ❑ | ❑ |
| 2 Are you a ruthless person? | ❑ | ❑ | ❑ |
| 3 Do you like going to interviews? | ❑ | ❑ | ❑ |
| 4 Do you like hard work? | ❑ | ❑ | ❑ |
| 5 Do you impress people? | ❑ | ❑ | ❑ |
| 6 Do you practise at your favourite sport? | ❑ | ❑ | ❑ |
| 7 Do you sit on committees? | ❑ | ❑ | ❑ |
| 8 Do you envy successful people? | ❑ | ❑ | ❑ |
| 9 Would you like to be manager of your section at work? | ❑ | ❑ | ❑ |
| 10 Do you like your job? | ❑ | ❑ | ❑ |

|  | Yes | Don't know | No |
|---|---|---|---|
| 11 Do you wake up feeling tired? | ❏ | ❏ | ❏ |
| 12 Do you discuss your work with friends or family? | ❏ | ❏ | ❏ |
| 13 Are you a stickler for routine? | ❏ | ❏ | ❏ |
| 14 Would you retire if you won the Lottery? | ❏ | ❏ | ❏ |
| 15 Do you motivate people? | ❏ | ❏ | ❏ |
| 16 Do you try to impress people? | ❏ | ❏ | ❏ |
| 17 Are you satisfied that you will get promotion in the near future? | ❏ | ❏ | ❏ |
| 18 Do you plan your week ahead? | ❏ | ❏ | ❏ |
| 19 Would you be angry if a colleague obtained promotion? | ❏ | ❏ | ❏ |
| 20 Do you save money for the future? | ❏ | ❏ | ❏ |
| 21 Do you like taking exams? | ❏ | ❏ | ❏ |
| 22 Would you work abroad? | ❏ | ❏ | ❏ |
| 23 Would you like to be a film star? | ❏ | ❏ | ❏ |
| 24 Do you like winning at games? | ❏ | ❏ | ❏ |
| 25 So far, have you had a successful life? | ❏ | ❏ | ❏ |

## Assessment

Award yourself 2 points for each *yes* answer, 1 point for each *don't know* answer and 0 points for each *no* answer.

### Less than 17 points

Power, status and riches are not the most important things in your life and you do not look upon success as being necessary to achieve happiness.

As long as you and your family are happy and contented, you are satisfied with your lot.

### 18–35 points

You are in the happy position of being quite content with your lot.

You do not particularly aspire to obtaining high positions in life and are satisfied with a reasonable performance at work as long as this provides a steady income and security for you and your family.

### 36–50 points

You are likely to be very successful in your chosen profession, and this is extremely important to you.

You are not afraid of hard work and you have the ability and motivation to make a success of any undertaking.

# Leader

Tick the appropriate column.

|  |  | Yes | Don't know | No |
|---|---|:---:|:---:|:---:|
| 1 | Do you rise early in the morning? | ❑ | ❑ | ❑ |
| 2 | Are you the life and soul at a party? | ❑ | ❑ | ❑ |
| 3 | Are you not nervous at meeting people? | ❑ | ❑ | ❑ |
| 4 | Are you a good organiser? | ❑ | ❑ | ❑ |
| 5 | Do you get restless at mundane tasks? | ❑ | ❑ | ❑ |
| 6 | Do you believe in honesty in business? | ❑ | ❑ | ❑ |
| 7 | Have you a stable family life? | ❑ | ❑ | ❑ |
| 8 | Do you work in the lunch break? | ❑ | ❑ | ❑ |
| 9 | Would you like to be in charge of an expedition? | ❑ | ❑ | ❑ |
| 10 | Have you ever been a manager in business? | ❑ | ❑ | ❑ |

|  |  | Yes | Don't know | No |
|---|---|:---:|:---:|:---:|
| 11 | Would you cancel a holiday if work requires you in an emergency? | ❏ | ❏ | ❏ |
| 12 | Do you have a second job? | ❏ | ❏ | ❏ |
| 13 | Do you always speak your mind? | ❏ | ❏ | ❏ |
| 14 | Do you always look smart at work? | ❏ | ❏ | ❏ |
| 15 | Would you take over at a car crash? | ❏ | ❏ | ❏ |
| 16 | Would you be comfortable leading other people? | ❏ | ❏ | ❏ |
| 17 | Are you a captain at sport? | ❏ | ❏ | ❏ |
| 18 | Are you good at debates? | ❏ | ❏ | ❏ |
| 19 | Are your always fair-minded? | ❏ | ❏ | ❏ |
| 20 | Are you often asked for your advice? | ❏ | ❏ | ❏ |
| 21 | Have you ever served on a committee? | ❏ | ❏ | ❏ |
| 22 | Do you like honest people? | ❏ | ❏ | ❏ |
| 23 | Do you get on well with subordinates? | ❏ | ❏ | ❏ |
| 24 | Would you like to be in politics? | ❏ | ❏ | ❏ |
| 25 | Are you a good public speaker? | ❏ | ❏ | ❏ |

## Analysis

The definition of a leader is anyone who holds the position of dominance, authority or influence in a group. In psychology, it is also applied to someone who possesses the necessary qualities to become such a leader.

There are many different types of leader, some of which can be categorised as follows:

*Authoritarian leader*   For example, a dictator, who has absolute authority and does not need to consult with other members of his group when making decisions. Examples of such dictators can be found in the military, industry, youth gangs and families.

*Democratic leader*   Leader who acts in accordance with the wishes of the group or organisation he represents.

*Nominal leader*   A figurehead, or leader in name only.

The qualities required to be a successful leader are many, and successful leadership behaviour depends to a great extent on the type of leadership situation. There is, therefore, no set of hard-and-fast rules as to what type of personality constitutes leadership capabilities. A great military leader, for example, must have organisational skills as well as the ability to motivate his troops, and the same can be said to apply to many leaders in industrial settings.

## Assessment

Award yourself 2 points for each *yes* answer, 1 point for each *don't know* answer and 0 points for each *no* answer.

## Less than 17 points

You do not appear to aspire to leadership and seem happy to go with the tide and let others take the initiative.

Because of this you are probably satisfied with your chosen profession and satisfied to lead a comfortable life without too much responsibility.

Should you wish to progress further in your chosen career, then it may be necessary to make the effort to assert yourself more. However, it is unlikely that this is your ultimate ambition and you are content to remain the hard-working grafter, happy with the niche in life that you have created.

While you might not reach the dizzy heights of leadership, your hard work could, nevertheless, bring you some unexpected promotion from time to time.

## 18–35 points

Although you exhibit good leadership qualities and are ready to take on tasks that other people may shirk, you are reluctant to push yourself forward, and are quite happy for others to take over the reins of responsibility.

With this outlook and attitude you are likely to lead a contented life without the often self-inflicted pressure of being better than the next person.

You are likely to be conscientious, patient, philosophical and a good team player who would make a good team leader, but only if the opportunity presented itself.

## 36–50 points

You exhibit great strength of character and leadership qualities. If you have not yet reached the heights in your chosen career, you have sufficient ambition, drive, determination and resilience to do so one day.

You are in your element when able to organise and lead from the front, and find it frustrating when someone else is taking over the reins instead of yourself.

You can be something of a workaholic, however, and are able to deal with a heavy workload, which you take in your stride.

Although you have total confidence in your own ability, you should also be mindful of the fact that most of us need the co-operation of others in order to succeed. Often, consultation is as much an important part of strong leadership as expecting people to follow your lead unquestioningly.

# Confidence

Tick the appropriate column.

| | Yes | Don't know | No |
|---|---|---|---|
| 1 Would you take part in a television quiz show? | ❑ | ❑ | ❑ |
| 2 Would you be confident about being best man at a wedding? | ❑ | ❑ | ❑ |
| 3 Are you a very positive person? | ❑ | ❑ | ❑ |
| 4 Would you like to fly a plane? | ❑ | ❑ | ❑ |
| 5 Would you like to meet Royalty? | ❑ | ❑ | ❑ |
| 6 Have you ever argued with a superior? | ❑ | ❑ | ❑ |
| 7 Would you care if friends saw you naked? | ❑ | ❑ | ❑ |
| 8 Would you argue with a traffic warden if you thought you were right? | ❑ | ❑ | ❑ |

| | Yes | Don't know | No |
|---|---|---|---|
| 9 Do you believe that 'attack' is the 'best form of defence'? | ❏ | ❏ | ❏ |
| 10 Are you confident driving in heavy traffic? | ❏ | ❏ | ❏ |
| 11 Are you confident when crossing roads? | ❏ | ❏ | ❏ |
| 12 Would you go on ferries in rough weather? | ❏ | ❏ | ❏ |
| 13 Are you sometimes inclined to be ruthless? | ❏ | ❏ | ❏ |
| 14 Are you unafraid of persons in authority? | ❏ | ❏ | ❏ |
| 15 Do you ignore warning signs? | ❏ | ❏ | ❏ |
| 16 Would you take on a more difficult occupation? | ❏ | ❏ | ❏ |
| 17 Would you like to appear live on a television talk show? | ❏ | ❏ | ❏ |
| 18 Do you think you are cleverer than average? | ❏ | ❏ | ❏ |
| 19 Would you direct a play on stage? | ❏ | ❏ | ❏ |
| 20 Would you be confident enough to drive in a car rally? | ❏ | ❏ | ❏ |

|  | Yes | Don't know | No |
|---|---|---|---|
| 21  Would you walk through a cemetery at night? | ❏ | ❏ | ❏ |
| 22  Would you fly in a micro-light aircraft? | ❏ | ❏ | ❏ |
| 23  Would you like to be a politician? | ❏ | ❏ | ❏ |
| 24  Would you walk on a tight rope? | ❏ | ❏ | ❏ |
| 25  Would you tackle a burglar? | ❏ | ❏ | ❏ |

## Definition

There are three definitions of confidence, as explained below. It is the first of these definitions that is being tested in this exercise.

1  assuredness and self-reliance in one's own abilities

2  belief in another person's trustworthiness or competency

3  an agreement that information is not to be divulged, as in the phrase, *in confidence*.

## Assessment

Award yourself 2 points for each *yes* answer, 1 point for each *don't know* answer and 0 points for each *no* answer.

### Less than 17 points

You appear to have very little confidence in your own abilities.

This may be because you are of a somewhat nervous disposition or that you are over-modest about your achievements, even to the extent of running yourself down at times.

Despite the fact that many people admire modesty, especially in high-achievers, it might be a good idea sometimes to evaluate just what you have achieved in life, and what talents you possess, compared with other people who seem much more confident than yourself. You may surprise yourself by such an analysis as to just how much you have going for you, and it may make you believe more in your own abilities in the future.

If your lack of confidence is due to nervousness in meeting people, especially when in the company of groups of people, then you should make an effort to mix with other people more. If possible, play to your strengths, for example, if you are a good chess player, then join a chess club, or if you want to learn a foreign language, then enrol in a course at your local polytechnic.

If you can gain more confidence, it will, in turn, encourage more people to have confidence in you, with the result that you could achieve much more success in life.

## 18–35 points

You appear to be a quietly confident person who is prepared to take a few risks in your life, although generally you prefer security without taking too many chances.

While you have confidence in your own abilities, you are careful not to be over-confident and this enables you to make decisions in a careful and structured manner after weighing up all the options.

## 36–50 points

You are a very confident, positive person and have almost total belief in anything you do. You would be of great value in an emergency.

Because you are so assured and self-reliant, you are someone who likes to get involved with anything that is happening around you. For example, if there was a complete reorganisation at your place of work you would want to be involved in the organisation, make a good impression and hope that the reorganisation might provide you with a better career opportunity. In a similar situation, a less confident person might be quite alarmed and fear that the reorganisation might lead to redundancies or changes in their job description.

The only need for caution as far as you are concerned is the danger of over-confidence. This could result in you taking unnecessary risks, or being seen by others as brash or cocky.

Also, remember that success is something that needs to be worked hard for. It will not happen just because you expect it to.

# Aggression

Tick the appropriate column.

| | Yes | Don't know | No |
|---|---|---|---|
| 1  Have you ever been involved in a fight? | ❏ | ❏ | ❏ |
| 2  Do you play contact sports? | ❏ | ❏ | ❏ |
| 3  Have you a strong will to win? | ❏ | ❏ | ❏ |
| 4  Do you frequently lose your temper? | ❏ | ❏ | ❏ |
| 5  Are you a bad loser? | ❏ | ❏ | ❏ |
| 6  Do you always try to get your own way? | ❏ | ❏ | ❏ |
| 7  Have you ever cheated? | ❏ | ❏ | ❏ |
| 8  Do you get involved in road rages? | ❏ | ❏ | ❏ |
| 9  Would you fight back if attacked by a mugger? | ❏ | ❏ | ❏ |

|  | Yes | Don't know | No |
|---|---|---|---|
| 10 Do you use bad language frequently? | ❏ | ❏ | ❏ |
| 11 Would you tackle a burglar? | ❏ | ❏ | ❏ |
| 12 Do you think that you are ruthless? | ❏ | ❏ | ❏ |
| 13 Do you like action films? | ❏ | ❏ | ❏ |
| 14 Would you obey an order if you thought that it were unreasonable? | ❏ | ❏ | ❏ |
| 15 Have you ever browbeaten a person weaker than yourself? | ❏ | ❏ | ❏ |
| 16 Would you make a citizen's arrest? | ❏ | ❏ | ❏ |
| 17 Is aggressive behaviour sometimes necessary as a means to an end? | ❏ | ❏ | ❏ |
| 18 Do you watch boxing? | ❏ | ❏ | ❏ |
| 19 Would you remonstrate with a person using bad language in a public place? | ❏ | ❏ | ❏ |
| 20 Do you believe that attack is the best form of defence? | ❏ | ❏ | ❏ |
| 21 In a war, would you kill the enemy? | ❏ | ❏ | ❏ |
| 22 If there were a war, would you like to be a fighter pilot? | ❏ | ❏ | ❏ |

|  | Yes | Don't know | No |
|---|---|---|---|
| 23  If a person played a trick upon you, would you try to get your own back? | ❑ | ❑ | ❑ |
| 24  If you wanted something badly, would you leave no stone unturned until you got it? | ❑ | ❑ | ❑ |
| 25  Would you complain about a dog always barking? | ❑ | ❑ | ❑ |

## Analysis

In humans, aggression is a general term used for a wide variety of acts including attack or hostility towards one another, and this can be caused by such factors as fear or frustration, a desire to produce fear or flight in others and a tendency to impose one's ideas or interests on others.

In humans, learned experience is important in determining the level of aggressive behaviour and generally the trading of insults or the presence of weapons has been learned from various sources.

The obtaining of rewards by children, such as toys, attention and sweets, as a result of aggressive behaviour is also likely to be repeated. Children also learn aggression by observing others, by having role models and by the influence of the mass media.

In general, the kind of aggression that most people tend to think of when the term is used is aggression evoked by frustration or the thwarting of one's goals. It is also typified by a display of the will for power and the desire to control others

## Assessment

Award yourself 2 points for each *yes* answer, 1 point for each *don't know* answer and 0 points for each *no* answer.

### Less than 17 points

You have an extremely passive, non-aggressive nature and rarely become upset at other people's actions, or when things do not appear to be going the way you wish.

While this means that you are likely to go through life without upsetting anyone and are likely to make many friends, it can also mean that you are sometimes taken advantage of, and in certain circumstances bullied. It may be necessary to try to toughen up just a little, while still retaining your charm and placid nature, if you are to realise many of your ambitions and aspirations.

Try to assert yourself a little more.

### 18–35 points

While knowing what you want out of life, you have a sufficiently balanced temperament to enable you to achieve this without walking over everyone else in order to fulfil your ambitions.

Although you are generally passive, when someone takes advantage of you, you are able to make a stand against them and are capable of calling on a degree of measured aggression just at the right time, when it is necessary. If, on the rare occasions you do go too far and lose your temper, you are likely to regret it later.

### 36–50 points

Your score indicates that you are of a very aggressive nature, and this aggression can even be *the* dominant force in your personality.

It is thus important that you make a serious attempt to temper this aggression, which may include the need to have more consideration for others. One way to do this is to try and put yourself in the other person's position and see their point of view more. Also, bear in mind that one sure-fire way of losing an argument, and alienating people against you, is to lose your temper and become aggressive. In almost all situations, diplomacy is a much more effective approach than demand.

You should attempt to analyse your behaviour patterns and your reactions to certain situations to see if there are other ways of achieving your aspirations. It may also help you to relax more and get things into perspective by taking up creative or recreational therapeutic pursuits or hobbies, such as painting, writing or gardening.

Try counting to ten much more often whenever your feel your blood pressure rising.

# Section 2
# Aptitude tests

# Aptitude tests

## Introduction

This section consists of two separate intelligence tests designed to measure your verbal and numerical ability, reasoning skills and diagrammatical or spatial reasoning under strictly timed conditions.

Intelligence is the capacity to learn or understand. Although intelligence is possessed by all people, it varies in amount for each person, and remains the same throughout life from approximately 18 years of age.

In psychology, intelligence is defined as the capacity to acquire knowledge or understanding, and to use it in novel situations.

Intelligence quotient (IQ) is an age-related measure of intelligence and is defined as 100 times mental age. The word quotient means the result of dividing one quantity by another, and intelligence can be defined as mental ability and quickness of mind.

The earliest known attempts to rank people in terms of intelligence date back to the Chinese Mandarin system, at about 500 BC, when studying the works of Confucius enabled successful candidates to enter the public service. The top 1% of candidates were successful in progressing to the next stage, where they would again be run off against each other, and the procedure repeated yet again through a final layer of selection. Thus, the chosen candidates were in the top 1% of the top 1% of the top 1%.

The first modern intelligence test was devised in 1905 by the French psychologists Alfred Binet and Theodore Simon. The pair developed a 30-item test with the purpose of ensuring that no child be denied admittance to the Paris school system without formal examination.

In 1916, the American psychologist Lewis Terman revised the Binet–Simon scale to provide comparison standards for Americans from age three to adulthood. Terman devised the term *intelligence quotient* and developed the so-called Stanford–Binet intelligence test to measure IQ after joining the faculty of Stanford University as professor of education. The Stanford–Binet test was further revised in 1937 and 1960 and remains today one of the most widely used of all intelligence tests.

An IQ test is, by definition, any test that purports to measure intelligence. Generally, such tests consist of a series of tasks, each of which has been standardised with a large representative population of individuals. Such a procedure establishes the average IQ as 100.

When measuring the IQ of a child, that child is given an intelligence test that has already been given to thousands of other children, and an average score has been established for each age group. Thus, a child who at 8 years of age obtained a result expected of a 10 year old would score an IQ of 125, that figure being mental age divided by chronological age × 100, or 10/8 × 100. On the other hand, a child of 10 years of age who obtained a result expected of an 8 year old would score an IQ of 80, or 8/10 × 100.

Because mental age remains constant from the age of 18, this method of calculation does not apply to adults. Adults have, instead, to be judged on a standardised IQ test whose average score is 100, and the results graded above and below this score according to known scores.

With aptitude tests in particular, it is advantageous to familiarise yourself with the type of questions and recurring themes that you are likely to encounter and the tests that follow will provide valuable practice for readers who may have to take an IQ test in the future.

Because the tests have been specially compiled for this book, they have not been standardised, therefore, an actual IQ rating cannot be provided. We do, however, provide a guide to assessing your performance on each of the separate tests.

On all of the tests you have limited time, and this time limit should be strictly adhered to, otherwise your score will be invalidated. It is, therefore, important that you do not spend too much time on any one question; if in doubt, leave it and return to it using the time remaining. If you do not know an answer, it may be well worth while having an intuitive guess, since this may well prove to be correct.

# IQ test one

## Introduction

Test one consists of four sub-tests, each of 10 questions, in four different disciplines: spatial ability, logical thought processes, verbal ability and numerical ability.

A performance rating is provided following the answers at the end of the test. A rating is given for each sub-test of 10 questions to enable you to identify your own strengths or weaknesses and we also give an overall rating for the complete test of 40 questions. It is this overall rating which is the best guide to your performance.

There is a time limit of 30 minutes for each 10-question test and of 2 hours for the complete 40-question test. You should keep strictly within your time limit, otherwise your score will be invalidated.

## Spatial ability test

Read the instructions to each question and study each set of diagrams carefully.

1

Which set of circles comes next?

A          B          C          D

E          F

2

is to

as

is to

A          B          C          D          E

3 Which is the odd one out?

4

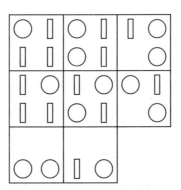

Which is the missing tile?

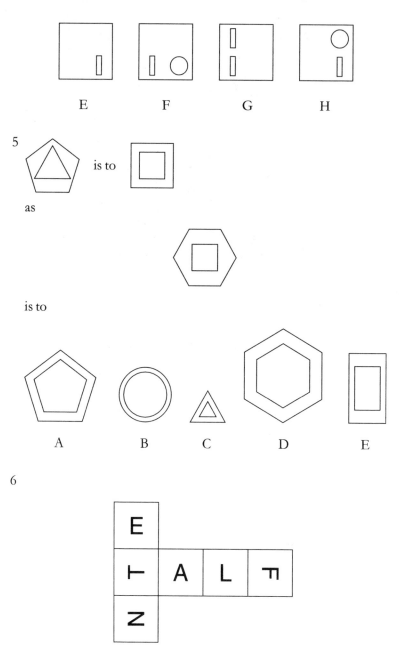

5

is to

as

is to

6

When the net on page 247 is folded to form a cube, which one of the following can be produced?

7

What comes next?

8 is to

as

is to

9

What comes next?

10

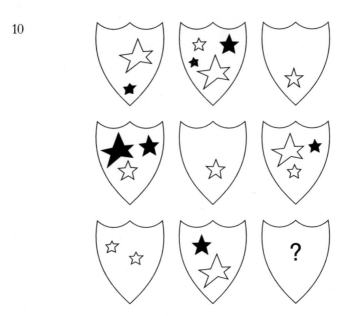

Which shield should replace the one with the question mark?

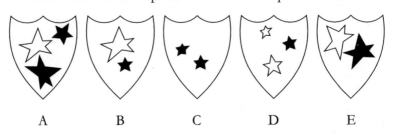

A       B       C       D       E

## Logic test

Calculators are not allowed, and are not considered necessary for this test.

1  What comes next?

CANASTA
ACTRESS
SAUSAGE
ESCAPED

Is it pagodas, develop, angular, doublet or cabaret?

2  What number should replace the question mark?

|   | 1 |   |   |   | 2 | 1 |
|---|---|---|---|---|---|---|
|   | 3 |   | 3 | 5 |   |   |
| 3 | 4 |   | 5 | 5 | 4 |   |
| 3 |   | 2 |   | ? |   | 2 |
| 2 |   |   |   |   | 4 |   |
| 3 |   | 3 | 3 | 4 |   | 2 |
| 2 | 3 |   | 3 |   | 2 |   |

3  What letter should replace the question mark?

| A | B | C | E | G | J |
|---|---|---|---|---|---|
| M | Q | U | Z | E | ? |

4  What number should replace the question mark?

76492, 28467, 76472, 26467, ?

5 Into which of the remaining two squares below would you place
   the letters H and I?

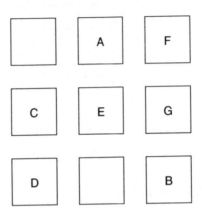

6 Carol beats Peter at golf but loses to Colin. Jill usually wins
   against Peter, sometimes against Carol but never against Colin.
   List the four players in order of ability.

7 Which is the odd one out?

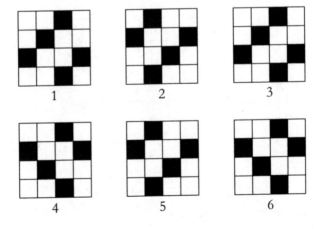

8  What number should replace the question mark?

| 3 | 13 | 8 | 7 | 9 |
|---|----|---|---|---|
| 4 | 7 | 2 | 5 | 6 |
| 9 | 5 | 6 | 11 | 1 |
| 10 | 17 | 14 | 16 | 9 |
| 2 | 6 | 2 | 3 | ? |

9  Which group of letters is the odd one out?

EDKJ       NMTS       IHON       TSYX       POVU

10  What number comes next?

3846721
4672183
7218364
?

## Verbal ability test

1  Change one letter only in each of the words below to produce a familiar phrase.

TAME FOOD CART ON

2  Which two of the following words are most opposite in meaning?

commendable, plausible, banal, unlikely, receptive, offensive

3  INSIDE is to MAGMA as OUTSIDE is to: sulphur, lava, crust, plate, earth, erupt

4  GLACIATED MAT is an anagram of which two words, 4 letters and 8 letters long, that are opposite in meaning?

5  Which word in brackets is most similar in meaning to the word in capitals?

PENITENT (pervasive, apologetic, impecunious, callous, invasive)

6  Only one set of five letters below can be arranged to spell out a 5-letter English word. Find the word.

BLEIT
TONTE
TIUNP
GNEUR
HEMUT

7

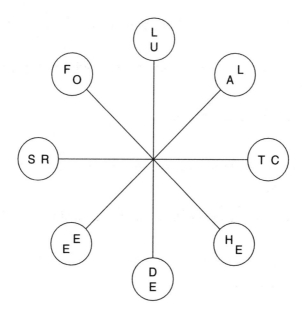

Find two 8-letter words that have opposite meanings by reading clockwise around the diagram above and, for each word, taking one letter at a time from each circle. Each word starts at a different circle, but all letters in each word are in the correct order. Use each letter once only.

8 What is the meaning of assiduous?

a) living a strict life
b) forceful
c) persevering
d) ingenious
e) harsh or acidic

9 Find a familiar phrase reading clockwise around the following diagram. You have to find the starting point and insert the missing letters. Only alternate letters are shown.

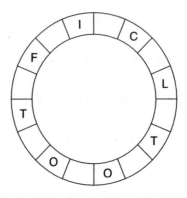

10 Work from letter to adjacent letter horizontally and vertically, but not diagonally, to spell out a 12-letter word. Use each letter once only. You have to find the starting point, and provide the missing letters.

| | | | |
|---|---|---|---|
| N | E | I | R |
| * | N | E | E |
| E | I | * | P |

## Numerical ability test

Calculators may be used in this test, if preferred.

1  Michael has £72.00 to spend. He spends 2/3 on computer
   software, then 0.375 of what he has left on lunch and finally £6.00
   on a taxi home. What is his financial situation at the end of the
   day?

2  A merchant had six barrels of different sizes. They contained 15,
   16, 18, 19, 20 and 31 litres respectively. Five of the barrels are full
   of wine and only one is full of water.

   The first customer bought two barrels of wine and the second
   customer bought twice as much wine as the first. The merchant
   returned home with the barrel of water. How much did it
   contain?

3  How many minutes is it before 12 noon, if 44 minutes ago it was
   three times as many minutes past 9 a.m.?

4  Three brothers joined the army on the same day.

   Alf comes home once every 5 days, Sid comes home once every
   4 days and Jim comes home once every 11 days. How often will all
   three meet up together?

5  What number should replace the question mark?

  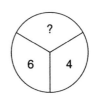

6  Three friends were playing poker.

   Each player had a certain amount of money, in addition to which there was a pool of money in the centre of the table.

   Alan said: *If I win this pool I will have twice as much money as both of you put together*
   Bernice said: *If I win this pool I will have three times as much money as both of you put together*
   Carol said: *If I win this pool I will have five times as much money as both of you put together*

   How much money was in the pool and how much money had each player?

7  What number continues the sequence?

   1        5        19        77        307        ?

8  A snail is climbing out of a well that is 10 feet deep. Every hour the snail climbs up 3 feet and slides back down 2 feet. How many hours will it take for the snail to escape from the well?

9  What number continues the sequence?

   368, 406, 452, 494, 538, ?

10 Harry has a third as many again as Larry, who has a third as many again as Barry. Altogether they have 222.

   How many does each one have?

# Answers to IQ test one

## *Spatial ability test*

1 D: the single larger circles are getting smaller. The smaller circles in between are increasing in number by one each time and getting larger from the bottom.

2 D: only lines which appear in the same position just twice in the first three squares are transferred to the final square. Only circles which appear in the same position just once are transferred.

3 F: A is the same as D, C is the same as G and B is the same as E.

4 E: looking both across and down, only when the same figure appears in the same position in the first two squares is it transferred to the third square. However, circles then become rectangles and vice versa.

5 A: the number of sides on the outside figure decreases by one, but the number of sides on the inside figure increases by one.

6 E.

7 B: The black dot appears in the first square and every subsequent third square. Every third square contains a white circle. The horizontal line at the top appears in the first square and every subsequent fourth square. Every alternate square contains a diagonal line and a vertical line.

8 B: a quarter is added to the largest and smallest arcs moving clockwise. A quarter is added to the middle arc moving anti-clockwise.

9 D: the circle moves one corner anti-clockwise at each stage, and the diagonal line moves two pairs of corners clockwise at each stage.

10 A: each horizontal and vertical line of shields contains three black stars and four white stars.

## Logic test

1 develop: each word starts with the last and first letters, in that order, of the previous word.

2 4: each number represents the number of digits that are adjacent to it either horizontally, vertically or diagonally.

3 K: the sequence runs –
ABCdEfGhiJklMnopQrstUvwxyZabcdEfghijK

4 76452: reverse and deduct one from the same number each time, i.e. the number next to the 2.

5

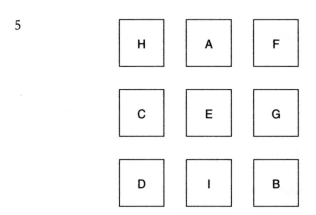

Replace each letter with its corresponding number in the alphabet to form a magic square in which each horizontal, vertical and corner-to-corner line totals 15.

6  Colin is the strongest, followed by Carol, then Jill, then Peter.

7  2: all the others are a mirror image of their neighbour looking across and down.

8  5: looking across and down, in each line the sum of alternate numbers total the same, for example, in the first line across,
$3 + 8 + 9 = 13 + 7$ (20)

9  TSYX: reverse the first two and the last two letters in each group. The sequence then progresses 2 consecutive letters, miss 4, then 2 consecutive, for example, EDKJ becomes DE****JK.

10  1836427: each number starts with the last five digits of the previous number, followed by the first two digits reversed.

## Verbal ability test

1  take good care of

2  plausible, unlikely

3  lava

4  calm, agitated

5  apologetic

6  TUINP = input

7  desolate, cheerful

8  c)  persevering

9 out of circulation

10 inexperience

## Numerical ability test

1 £9 left: £72 less 2/3 = £24. 0.375 × £24 = £9 i.e. £15 left less
£6 = £9

2 20 litres

| First customer | Second customer |
|---|---|
| 15 | 16 |
| <u>18</u> | 19 |
| 33 | <u>31</u> |
| | 66 |

3 34 minutes: 12 noon − 34 minutes = 11.26 a.m.

9 a.m. + (34 × 3) = 102 minutes = 10.42 a.m.
11.26 − 10.42 = 44 minutes

4 Once every 220 days (5 × 4 × 11)

5 2: 6 × 4 = 24/12 = 2. Similarly, 3 × 20 = 60/12 = 5

6 Pool = £15
Alan = £1
Bernice = £3
Carol = £5

7 1229: the sequence runs × 4 + 1 and × 4 − 1 alternately

8  8 hours: after 1 hour it has climbed one foot. After 7 hours it has climbed 7 feet. In the eighth hour it climbs the remaining 3 feet and is at the top, so does not slide back.

9  596: add the number formed by the first and last digits each time, so **538** + 58 = 596

10  Barry = 54, Larry = 72, Harry = 96

## Performance rating

Each 10-question test

| | |
|---|---|
| 10 | exceptional |
| 8−9 | excellent |
| 7 | very good |
| 5−6 | good |
| 4 | average |

Complete 40-question test

| | |
|---|---|
| 36−40 | exceptional |
| 31−35 | excellent |
| 25−30 | very good |
| 19−24 | good |
| 14−18 | average |

# IQ test two

## Introduction

Test two consists of a battery of 20 questions in a variety of different disciplines: spacial ability, logical thought processes, verbal ability and numerical ability. A performance rating is provided following the answers at the end of the test.

A time limit of 60 minutes is allowed for completing the 20 questions. You should keep strictly within your time limit, otherwise your score will be invalidated.

Calculators may be used where preferred.

1 Which is the odd one out?

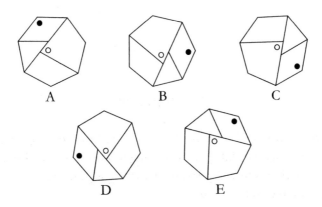

A          B          C

D          E

2 Which word in brackets is most opposite to the word in capitals?

IRRATIONAL (concerned, circumspect, regular, purposed, indelible)

3 What are the next two numbers in the sequence below?

1.5, 12.5, 3.25, 10.75, 5, 9, 6.75, 7.25

4 Which two words are most opposite in meaning?

large, hopeful, wizened, fatuous, turgid, healthy

5 Insert the numbers 1–6 in the circles on page 266 so that for any particular circle the sum of the numbers in the circles connected directly to it equals the value corresponding to the number in that circle as given in the list.

Example:

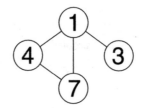

$1 = 14\ (4 + 7 + 3)$
$4 = 8\ (7 + 1)$
$7 = 5\ (4 + 1)$
$3 = 1$

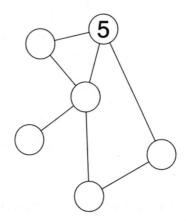

$1 = 9$
$2 = 6$
$3 = 11$
$4 = 7$
$5 = 10$
$6 = 14$

6

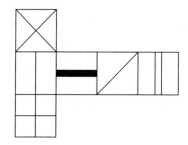

When the above is folded to form a cube, which one of the following can be produced?

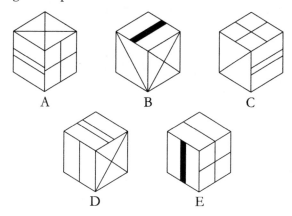

A          B          C

D          E

7  Which two words below are closest in meaning?

quiddity, espousal, effluence, tension, support, literate

8  What numbers should replace the question marks?

| 7 | 6 | 2 | 5 | 1 |
|---|---|---|---|---|
| 8 | 9 | 6 | 3 | 2 |
| 1 | 7 | 8 | 6 | 1 |
| 2 | 4 | 7 | 3 | 1 |
| 9 | 1 | 6 | 6 | 1 |
| 2 | 5 | 3 | ? | ? |

9

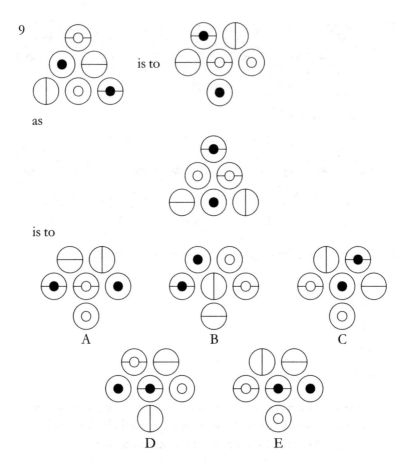

10 DISCLAIM is to REPUDIATE as ABDURE is to: waive, forsake, forgo, forfeit, renounce?

11 What numbers should replace the question marks?

12

What comes next?

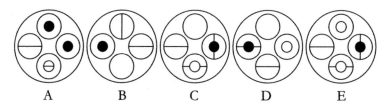

|     |     |     |     |     |
|-----|-----|-----|-----|-----|
|  A  |  B  |  C  |  D  |  E  |

13  Which of the following is *not* an anagram of a country?

hug yarn

teen pun

ink pasta

big mule

into sea

14  A batsman is out for 68 runs which raises his batting average for
the season from 32 to 36. How many runs would he have had to
have scored to raise his average for the season to 39?

15  Find the starting point and follow the instructions to arrive at the
treasure, marked **T**. Visit *every* square, but only once.

| 1E 2S | 2S 1E | 1S 2W |
|-------|-------|-------|
| **T** | 1S 1W | 2W 1N |
| 1N 2E | 2N 1E | 1N 1W |

1E
2S        means one square east, then two squares south

16

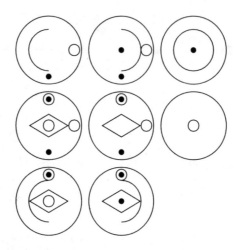

Which is the missing circle?

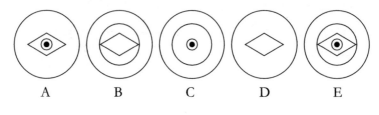

A          B          C          D          E

17  A        B        C        D        E        F        G        H

What letter is two to the left of the letter which comes immediately to the right of the letter which comes four to the left of the letter which comes two to the right of the letter E?

18  Change one letter only from each of the words below to produce a familiar phrase.

POUT ON CALF

19  Each of the nine squares opposite, marked 1A to 3C, incorporates all the lines and symbols which are shown in the squares of the same letter and number immediately above and to the left. For

example, 2B should incorporate all the lines and symbols contained in 2 and B.

However, one of the squares is incorrect. Can you find it?

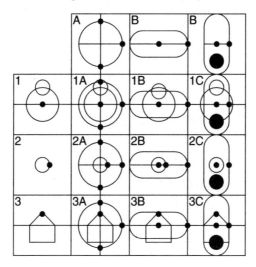

20

Barry lives 4 miles west of Alice
Carol lives 3 miles south of Barry
David lives 2 miles west of Carol
Elizabeth lives 1 mile north of David
Fiona lives 3 miles east of Elizabeth
Gareth lives 4 miles north of Fiona
Harry lives 1 mile west of Gareth.

How far, and in what direction, does Harry live from Barry?

## Answers to IQ test two

1  B: the rest are the same figure rotated.

2  circumspect

3  8.5 and 5.5: there are two sequences beginning with 1.5 and 12.5. The first increases by 1.75 and the second reduces by 1.75

4  wizened, turgid

5

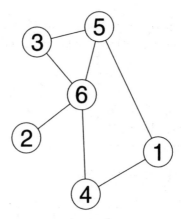

6  B

7  espousal, support

8  0    1

In each line add the first three numbers, then reverse the answer to obtain the last two numbers. So, $2 + 8 + 3 = 10$ which reversed $= 01$

9  E: the symbols change positions exactly as in the first analogy, for example, the symbol bottom left moves to top right.

10  forsake

11  27 and 10: $3 \times 9 = 27$ and $8 + 2 = 10$

12  C: looking across the top circle alternates dot/empty, the left
circle alternates empty/horizontal line, the right circle alternates
black dot with horizontal line/black dot/black dot with vertical
line, and the bottom circle alternates white dot with vertical
line/white dot with internal horizontal line/white dot with
horizontal line.

13  teen pun = Neptune. The countries are Hungary = hug yarn,
Pakistan = ink pasta, Belgium = big mule and Estonia = into sea

14  95

8 innings average 32 = 256
9 innings average 36 = 324
9 innings average 39 = 351

$256 + 68 = 324$; $256 + 95 = 351$

15

| 6 | 1 | 8 |
|---|---|---|
| T | 3 | 5 |
| 4 | 7 | 2 |

16  C: looking both across and down, only symbols that appear once
only in the same position in the first two circles are carried
forward to the third circle.

17  B

18  port of call

19  2C

20  2 miles North

## Performance rating

| | |
|---|---|
| 19–20 | exceptional |
| 16–18 | excellent |
| 13–15 | very good |
| 10–12 | good |
| 7–9 | average |